ROCK ART AND RITUAL
MINDSCAPES OF PREHISTORY

ROCK ART AND RITUAL
MINDSCAPES OF PREHISTORY

BRIAN A. SMITH & ALAN A. WALKER

AMBERLEY

From Alan:
I dedicate this book to Christine Mark and Jane Shutt
for their encouragement and belief in our project.
Also to Meg, Jack, Jude and Mist – my four-legged shadows.

From Brian:
I dedicate this book to my parents and to the late John Carter
– my art teacher – who taught me how to see!

First published 2011

Amberley Publishing
Cirencester Road, Chalford,
Stroud, Gloucestershire GL6 8PE

www.amberleybooks.com

British Library Cataloguing in Publication Data.
A catalogue record for this book is available from the British Library.

ISBN 978-1-4456-0188-5

Typesetting and Origination by Amberley Publishing.
Printed in Great Britain.

Contents

Preface

During our research, a number of common factors have been identified. These we have attempted to examine and interpret as objectively as possible. In some cases a subjective approach was unavoidable. This is not deliberate avoidance, as we wish to place our observations into an open arena for other researchers to verify, disprove or refine. Only by laying all our cards on the table will it be possible to reach safe and credible conclusions.

Ronald Morris, a retired solicitor and pioneering researcher, certainly did just this in his publications (1977, 1979) concerning Scottish and Manx rock art. He observed a relationship between the carvings, direct sunlight and watercourses. He also noted that most carved stones are on near-horizontal surfaces, and that where they occur, radial grooves from the centres of cup and ring markings almost always slope down the stone. Independently, we have made the same observations, and a great deal more. Such phenomena are key elements in our interpretations of prehistoric rock art within this second volume of *Rock Art and Ritual*. We have progressively built on such observations and presented arguments that we hope will stimulate further discussion and research.

Denied rainfall and rays from the sun, the Earth would be a dead planet. At least 5,000 years ago, the Neolithic inhabitants of the British Isles were only too aware of the fundamental importance of these elements to the continuity and sustainability of life. Both water and energy from sunlight were seen as being transferred from the sky (the upper layer of their cosmos) to the Earth's surface. This may seem an obvious statement of fact, but in times before scientific knowledge, such a transfer may well have been endowed with properties akin to sexual fertilisation.

In our first volume, we argued that the importance of such sky–land transfer was expressed as motifs carved in stone, which without metal tools was the result of many hours of painstaking work. Not all rock carvings, it must be stressed, were symbols of this transfer; some probably had calendrical and other functions. For instance, 'calendar' stones appear to have been linked with either key rising or setting positions of the sun on a distant horizon, and the agency of the moon was exploited by rock-carved counting or calculating devices. Even here it is likely that the cosmos was seen as being integral to such activities, and that these appear to have continued into the Early Bronze Age.

The authors have taken the cosmological/life argument much further than in our first book. We have attempted to decipher various forms of rock art – seeking their symbolic and allegorical content from Ireland to Northern England, Cornwall to Scotland. We believe that we come close to achieving a better understanding of the 'architecture' of the Prehistoric Cosmos. Rock art shows remarkable consistency in its visual 'language', although there are local variations in style and concept. Such consistency could not have been the result of pure chance.

Our hypotheses constantly move through transition zones between external reality and the reality of the prehistoric mind. It appears that, especially during the Neolithic, things, places and events were perceived at more than one level: a stone axe-head was far more than a tool, a river more than flowing water, sunrise and sunset profoundly more than the beginning and end of a day. This occurs in twenty-first-century western society of course: a motor car is more than just a mode of transport, a dove is also a symbol for peace, the cross carries with it massive religious connotations. Teasing out the meaning of Neolithic symbolism and allegory was thought by many to be beyond recovery. Perhaps this volume represents a significant breakthrough.

Within these pages, the reader will encounter information in both written and graphic form. In many ways the most powerful is expressed visually. Even since the publication of our first volume of *Rock Art and Ritual* in 2008, advances in digital photography have enabled us to produce images that record the 'world out there' in ever more realistic detail. Many books show rock art as purely two-dimensional drawings, the result of converting rock rubbings into a graphic form suitable for publication. Although such recordings have been immensely important in combination with photographs and site location details, they may have inadvertently blocked the enquiring mind from seeing the essentially three-dimensional nature of rock art, and as a result, its purpose or meaning.

Considering the structure of this volume, we decided to divide the information into four sections. In part one, 'Of Rain and of Water', and part two, 'Of Rays and the Sun', we explore the relationship that Neolithic and Early Bronze Age cultures had with water and sunlight. Overlap does occur here. Prehistoric people did not sit down to write a book and neatly place their world into one or other of such categories. Always, we are dealing with a twenty-first-century interpretation of a prehistoric mindset. The closer we seem to be at 'gaining a handle' on prehistoric meaning and purpose, the more elusive definitive data becomes. Nevertheless, the book does follow two separate channels of investigation, as described above, in order to concentrate in detail on the individual merits of arguments relating to both water and the sun. Incredibly, both lines of enquiry converge in interpretations that appear to point towards a single concept, seen as an integral part of the same cosmic equation.

Part three, chapter nine, draws on details explored in parts one and two in an attempt to decipher specific kinds of rock art, chiefly within Northern England. Chapter ten deals with the possible ways in which prehistoric travellers found their way around the landscape, and how areas of landscape may have become ritualised.

Part four is the result of Alan A. Walker's observations and research over a number of years. Chapter eleven is a focused appraisal of the tors and basins and associated prehistoric monuments on Bodmin Moor, Cornwall. Chapter twelve returns to rock art, re-examining its context within the open landscape and within monuments. We also consider the function and purpose of certain monuments and their chronology. This chapter shares common ground with chapters nine and ten, but with a different emphasis: it takes a cognitive approach.

At the end of the book, we offer two speculative appendices, which should be read as marking the outer limit of this book's investigations. The contents seem to us to follow intuitively from the assertions we make in the main part of *Mindscapes of Prehistory*, but are not intended to be conclusive; rather, they are a starting point for future research.

METHODOLOGY

Unless otherwise stated, the photographic plates within the book are those of the authors. Currently we use digital cameras. Some photographs were taken on 35 mm film. Adobe Photoshop software was used in image manipulation and the creation of all the graphics. All of our images of rock art were obtained using non-invasive methods. Emphasis of certain marks on rocks was achieved using digital overlays.

Ordnance Survey grid references were recorded with hand-held Garmin GPS. The ten-figure readings may be considered as being accurate to within 10 m. True north was also established by using these instruments. If conventional magnetic or KVH digital compasses were used, corrections from magnetic north to true north were in accordance with current Ordnance Survey recommendations.

This book is the result of years of fieldwork, enquiry and contemplation. Is it possible that we have rediscovered the essential meaning, symbolism and purpose of much Neolithic rock art? The following pages are the distillation of our research.

REFERENCES

Morris, R. W. B., *The Prehistoric Rock Art of Argyll* (Poole: Dolphin Press, 1977).
Morris, R. W. B., *The Prehistoric Rock Art of Galloway and the Isle of Man* (Poole: Blanford Press, 1979).
Smith, B. A., and A. A. Walker, *Rock Art and Ritual: Interpreting the Prehistoric Landscapes of the North York Moors* (Stroud: Tempus, 2008).

PART ONE

OF RAIN AND OF WATER

Introduction to Part One

Progression through part one takes the reader from the pragmatic level of journeying by sea and inland by river to areas that are more speculative – with regard to water at a possible spiritual or cosmological level – during the Neolithic.

Prior to the phenomenal Neolithic expansion into the British Isles, Early Mesolithic hunter-gatherers crossed from Western Europe via land in 11,000–10,000 BP, soon after the retreat of the last ice sheet. The North Sea had not yet separated mainland Britain from the Continent.

These people initially made progress along the east coast of Britain, mainly exploiting seafood, as suggested today by the huge accumulations of seashell middens. They also hunted animals beside lakeside habitats, for example at Star Carr and at the Seamer Carrs in present-day North Yorkshire – now the peat remains of former glacier-dammed lakes.

Eventually they reached the west coast of Britain, shell middens again proving the mobility of these people and their ability to exploit the coastal fringes. Middens on the islands of the Inner Hebrides also prove their ability to cross by sea. Such crossings could have been made relatively easily with a canoe and by choosing the narrowest stretches of water, as Brian has proved on several occasions.

From the evidence of their built structures, artefacts and rock art, Neolithic people must have crossed far wider stretches of open sea in settlement ventures and for trade on a comparatively regular basis. They must have had quite large, sturdy seagoing vessels, although none have been discovered so far.

Barry Cunliffe, Professor of European Archaeology at the University of Oxford, writes the following under the heading 'The Offshore Islands: Britain and Ireland':

The spread of Neolithic ideas to Britain and Ireland must have involved sea journeys and the transportation, on a comparatively extensive scale, of domesticated breeding stock – cattle, sheep, goats and pigs – as well as the seed corn necessary to establish a sustainable agriculture … What is perhaps most dramatic is the apparent rate of progress through the islands. The Neolithic economy is first attested in the east of England, in Cambridgeshire, by *c.* 4300 BC. By 4000 BC it had reached Wales. A hundred years later it is found in Northern Ireland and by 3800 BC many parts of Scotland had been reached, including the islands of Orkney and Shetland in the far north. By any standards the spread was rapid – so rapid that we must suppose that the new ideas, and their necessary material back-up, were transmitted principally by sea. (Cunliffe 2008, 136)

Furthermore, we make the case that the sea and rivers may well have been revered (and feared) during the Neolithic. We also argue that rainfall, seen as the source of water, especially within early farming communities, was also revered. Indeed, some form of 'water-cult' unique to the British Isles may well have developed.

It was where the transfer of water at its purest occurs, between sky and earth in the hill country of the British Isles, that the majority of open-landscape rock art is to be found, often close to the sources of streams. These appear to have been special, even sacred, places where the nature of rock art in many instances appears to confirm that water and water-flow were of prime importance within the Neolithic belief system.

REFERENCE

Cunliffe, B., *Europe between the Oceans: 9000 BC–AD 1000* (London: Yale University Press, 2008).

1

Early Sea Adventurers

The Irish Sea in the Neolithic and early second millennium was not a barrier but a track-way across which people travelled freely, customs intertwined. Then, later, perhaps as the 'chiefdom' societies settled down in their small territories, the flux subsided (Burl 1979).

5,000 years before the Viking sagas related seafaring adventures of great daring to a home base in Scandinavia, and Norway in particular, adventurers were crossing wide expanses of open sea on a regular basis during the Neolithic period, now 6,000 years ago. Presumably in considerably inferior vessels to the clinker-built, state-of-the-art longships of the 'North Men', Neolithic seafarers made voyages between Atlantic Europe, Ireland and Britain, including to the Outer Hebrides, Orkneys and Shetlands. This is proved by evidence of trading and cultural links between settlements.

Most sea crossings during the Neolithic were probably made with a land destination in sight, in good visibility, at the height of summer (the Orkney Islands are visible from mainland Caithness, for example). No trace of seagoing boats has so far been discovered. Survivors, perhaps, of these early craft are still used in Wales and Ireland in the form of one-man circular coracles. Although far more seaworthy than a hollowed-out log boat, bigger craft with long hulls would have been needed in the open sea for transporting materials, animals and people and to give directional stability. Even so, wicker boats with stretched skins, shallow-drafted and unproven to have had any form of sail – and therefore possibly dependent on paddling or rowing – were pushing the technology of the time to its limits.

It is hard to believe, however, that such resourceful people failed to harness the wind via some form of sail configuration. Tentative evidence has recently come to light that such vessels were square-rigged, as were Bronze Age, Iron Age, Anglo-Saxon and Viking ships. Field walker Graham Hill discovered a fragment of slate in Paul parish, West Penwith, Cornwall, on a site where he was hoping to find Late Neolithic pottery and flintwork. The slate has a linear engraving that appears to depict a vessel with square rigging (*British Archaeology* 113, 9). Also, to quote Cunliffe from his article *People of the Sea*:

No hide boat has yet been found but the famous gold model from Broighter, Co. Derry, of a square-rigged vessel with provision for seven rowers and a steersman manning a steering oar to the rear quarter may represent just such a vessel from the 1st century BC. (Cunliffe 2002, pp. 14–15)

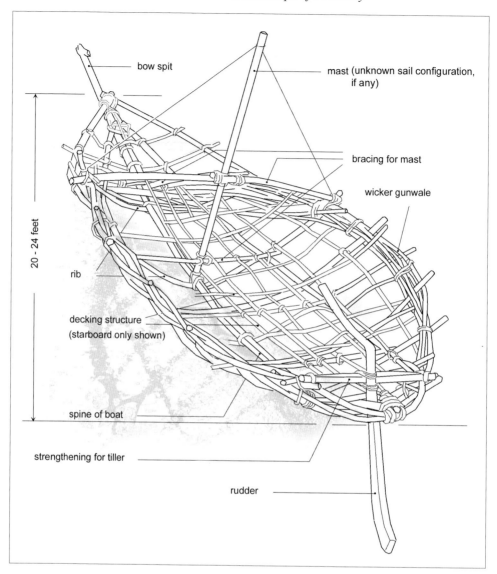

Fig. 1. Possible structure of a Neolithic seagoing craft.

Of course, this model is far more recent than the Neolithic period, but it may represent a continuation of tradition from that time. Such a design of vessel doesn't suddenly appear from nowhere.

Such craft may have set out in flotillas – several boats with women and children and domesticated animals, perhaps linked by ropes – in order to minimise risk should a capsize occur in all-out settlement ventures.

Willow and hazel may have been the preferred materials for constructing the boat frame because of their properties of strength and flexibility. A later Bronze Age boat excavated at Dover had oak planks 'sewn' together using twisted yew withies. Such bindings may also have secured the wicker frame of the Neolithic craft, and the beeswax and animal fat used in the Bronze Age boat may have waterproofed the stretched skins (see fig. 1 for the possible structural appearance of such a vessel – based on our scale model).

These Neolithic adventurers must have communicated in some way on returning to home base, possibly creating their own 'sagas' in order to persuade others to follow. Were journeys remembered in terms of direction, distance, time, landmarks and danger zones, which were then built into story form? Perhaps basic charts were carved into wood or stone or drawn onto pieces of bark or dried leather. As with the actual form of their seagoing boats, we can only postulate. Quoting Søren Thirslund from his book *Viking Navigation*, we may have a window into how this was achieved 4,000 years later:

> There is, however, one sailing direction, which claims for an exact direction finder. It is a sailing direction, from western Norway to southern Greenland, and it is so clearly described that it could be used to-day. Although translators disagree slightly at some points, the main directions are clear:
>
> 'FROM HERNAM IN NORWAY (near Bergen) STEER DUE WEST FOR HVARF IN GREENLAND (near Cape Farewell). YOU WILL THEN PASS HJALTLAND (The Shetland Islands) SO CLOSE THAT YOU MAY JUST SEE THEM IN CLEAR WEATHER, AND SO CLOSE TO THE FAROE ISLANDS THAT HALF OF THE MOUNTAIN IS UNDER THE WATER, AND SO CLOSE TO ICELAND THAT YOU MAY HAVE BIRDS AND WHALE FROM THERE.'
>
> These 1,400 nautical miles long voyages were probably started shortly after 1,000 AD and were continued for about 400 years. The sailing direction quoted above, learned and followed by rote until, centuries later, they were written down, must have given the safest and surest way to cross the featureless North Atlantic Ocean. (Thirslund 2007, 11)

Like the Vikings, deeds of great daring must have been exalted within Neolithic societies and perhaps became a driving force for trade and settlement over great distances, especially by sea. Heroes of the calibre of Eirik the Red, Bjarni Herjólfsson, Leif Eiriksson (the Lucky) and Thorfinn Karlsefni (the Valiant) must have existed and been role models for young adventurers of that time.

In order to undertake such journeys, Neolithic seafarers must have had sophisticated knowledge of tides and the phases of the moon, and an ability to establish (at least) the four cardinal points – north, east, south, west. The latter was probably achieved through an understanding of the apparent movement of the sun – consistently rising in the east, reaching its highest point in the sky when due south, and setting in the west. Importantly, the sun never 'journeys' into the north. Knowledge of where to locate the Pole Star may have been a guide on clear nights. Obviously, for greater accuracy, these observations were dependent on knowing the time of year and on the sun being visible. Sat nav has only just been made available in the twenty-first century for anyone to use. By triangulating a number of satellite signals, travellers can now navigate by land, sea or air, regardless of visibility conditions during day or night. The authors use GPS as a matter of course in recording and locating the ground positions of stones with rock art in frequently featureless tracts of moorland. Take away our high-tech systems and the enormity of the undertakings of Neolithic seafarers, with basic navigational abilities, becomes immediately apparent.

Why take such risks? What was driving these people to venture into the unknown? Already suggested is that theirs was a culture that exalted great daring. Was this the main force that drove these people to reach the extreme limits of the islands off Atlantic-facing Europe? It is not apparent that territory or land ownership (as we now know it) was a concept understood by the people of the Neolithic in the British Isles and, therefore, establishing new land was not the driving force. The process of sub-dividing and laying claim to areas of land seems to have started here in the Early Bronze Age. Undoubtedly, powerful chieftains/leaders were able to demand or persuade hundreds of people to give their time and energy to communal projects such as the construction of a cursus, henge, stone circle or sophisticated passage grave, even at their northern limits of settlement in the Orkney Islands. Was it the carrot rather than the stick that led to such immense communal undertakings? Perhaps they were sold to the populace as a benefit to all. Such structures would be meeting places where goods and ideas could be exchanged, deals made and social matters resolved. Of course, such events would almost certainly have been within strictly recognised and understood religious/spiritual parameters controlled by some form of elite, perhaps a shaman. Could these (religious) leaders have been instrumental in encouraging such risk-taking?

The Neolithic in the British Isles could be seen as a precursor of Viking events 4,000–5,000 years later. Both cultures appear to have revered daring exploits, enhanced no doubt in saga, myth and fable. These exploits led to expansion and settlement in both cultures, but neither seems to have developed the concept of land ownership as we know it today. Both had religious and cosmological views that were intimately tied into the natural world, where symbols for birth, life and death were all around. The sea was of paramount importance, both in the real world of survival and in the world of symbols and metaphors. This is a notion that will be developed in later chapters.

Rivers and lakes were also of great importance. Swedish Viking penetration into the heart of Europe, as far as the Black Sea, was achieved by navigating the great rivers of Eastern Europe. As a means of inland penetration and transportation, rivers were also important during the Neolithic in Britain, but rivers, lakes and water in general ran far deeper in the Neolithic mind and may have eventually lead to the creation of certain forms of rock art (col. pl. 1).

REFERENCES

Burl, A., *The Stone Circles of the British Isles* (London: Yale University Press, 1979).
Cunliffe, B., 'People of the Sea' in *British Archaeology* 63, pp. 14–15 (2002).
Hill, G., 'Cornish Stone Could Show Ancient Ship' in *British Archaeology* 113, p. 9 (2010).
Thirslund, S., *Viking Navigation* (Denmark: Viking Ship Museum, 2007).

2

Rivers, Streams and Lakes – Journeying Inland

To people familiar with boats and the sea, rivers would have afforded the obvious means of inland penetration. Conversely, to people travelling on land, rivers would have constituted major barriers to progress. Another difficulty encountered during the Neolithic, with regards to inland travel across vast areas of Britain and Ireland, would have been dense forests and areas of marshland, the latter being remnants from the last glaciation. Although Neolithic farmers were clearing areas of woodland, it was not until the Bronze Age, with its superior metal axes and obsession with land ownership, that substantial areas of forest began to be cleared.

Of course, inland penetration would only have been possible as far as the depth of water and other river conditions allowed. Should settlement within an area have been considered, boats specially designed for river travel would have been used. These may have included the dugout log boat or the ultra-lightweight coracle referred to in chapter one. The latter could easily have been portaged around obstacles by being carried on the back.

The River Tees, in North East England, was the former boundary between the North Riding of Yorkshire and County Durham to the north. On elevated ground overlooking the former tidal lower reaches of the Tees, now an area of marshland, stands Norton church. Within the grounds of the church, three Neolithic Cumbrian greenstone axeheads have been discovered. One is in perfect, unused condition. This suggests that the raised ground currently occupied by the church was possibly a sacred site during the Neolithic. Being close to tidal waters at that time, the site may have been approached by vessel from the sea (see 'The Bend in the Boyne' below).

The Tees was navigable to shallow-drafted seagoing vessels as far inland as Worsall, 22.5 km from the Tees estuary as the crow flies, even into the last century. The Ship public house, with a sailing ship on the signboard, seems strangely out of place in open countryside. Approximately 5 km further downstream, the former market town and trading port of Yarm occupies a bend in the River Tees. This was the first fording point inland from the river mouth at low tide until a stone bridge was built in 1400. Between Yarm and Worsall, on the north bank at Aislaby (Old Norse for Aslakr's village or homestead), the Vikings cut a slipway where they were able to pull their longships out of the river. The importance of rivers to travelling considerable distances inland is clear in the above example, even into recent history. Many rivers still have trading ports far inland.

The 'vik' in Viking is Old Norse for a trading settlement in a fjord, a glacier-deepened inlet from the sea, penetrating far inland, often into the mountainous interior of Norway. Examples of settlements in fjords and by rivers include Narvik (in a Norwegian fjord), Reykjavik (capital of Norse-settled Iceland) and Jorvik (the former Viking capital of England, now York on the River Ouse). Neolithic seafaring people probably had their own name for a settlement in a sea inlet, now lost or perhaps hidden within later names for settlements.

THE BEND IN THE BOYNE

Long before the pyramids were constructed beside the River Nile, Neolithic people constructed elaborate and massive passage tombs such as Knowth and Newgrange beside the River Boyne. Such structures would have required careful planning and the organisation of a large workforce. Materials for building Newgrange were in many cases from sources that were a considerable distance away, and such materials weighed heavy. Geraldine and Matthew Stout, in *Newgrange*, suggest that the huge kerbstones came from Clogher Head on the coast, 15 km north of the mouth of the Boyne. Granite cobbles, rounded by glaciers, have their origins in the Mourne Mountains, but were deposited by the ice in the Cooley Peninsula, 40 km north of the Boyne. The shiny white quartz above the eastern entrance is found only in the Wicklow Mountains, 70 km to the south (Stout and Stout 2008, p. 6) These and other source-specific stones were almost certainly transported along the coast and then up the Boyne in either wicker-framed boats with stretched cattle hides or on rafts of some form. Sleds were probably used to haul stone from their source to river or sea, and from the banks of the Boyne to the construction site.

SEEKING THE SOURCES OF RIVERS

Following a river, and eventually streams further inland, would have eventually meant abandoning any form of boat and resorting to travel on foot. Neolithic people may well have found tracks surviving from earlier people along the sides of riverbanks, on slopes above rivers and streams, or near the edges of lakes and marshland. In chapter two of the first volume of *Rock Art and Ritual*, we argued that the first pathways were probably created by herds of wild animals and that Early Mesolithic hunters adopted them in following their prey. This is likely to have occurred soon after the final retreat of the glaciers, around 10,000 years ago. Such routes would, no doubt, have led Neolithic people (still hunters as well as being early farmers) to the herds sought by earlier hunting parties. Rock motifs, usually simple cups, are to be found in several elevated locations in Northern England with linear distribution patterns, following lines of least effort, suggesting that they were carved beside ancient pathways. Currently, the consensus of opinion is that such stones, as with most open-air rock motifs, were carved during the Neolithic period.

Fig. 2. Which way?

Simple cups, without obvious arrangement, may approximate to the present-day arrow sign. Located beside pathways or corridors of movement, such stones may have offered a form of reassurance in what may well have been hostile environments. Tried and tested over generations, travellers could take some comfort in knowing they were following in the footsteps of their ancestors. Cupstones were more sophisticated than arrows (our symbol for indicating direction) in that they were bi-directional; they could be read either way around.

In the first volume of *Rock Art and Ritual*, we observed:

At the north-west corner of Rock 1, another small basin was cleaned to reveal a central countersunk cup. Water flow from this 'reservoir' divided into two natural channels before taking water over the highest (1.2 m) western edge of the rock. Once again, cups are found along the routes of both channels. (Smith and Walker 2008, 62)

Cups engraved into stones in relation to water were, in this example, almost certainly defining (even celebrating) directionality of water-flow. Arrows would not be needed in such instances as, of course, water can only flow downwards.

As mentioned above, and relating to the North York Moors and the Fylingdales Moors in particular, ancient pathways (recognised today as linear distributions of cupstones) frequently ran alongside elevated watercourses, or skirted the edges of former lakes or marshes. Crossing water was only as a last resort. Here marked stones have been found *in* watercourses on these moors in no less than eight instances. In conditions of poor visibility, it may well have been considered prudent to follow watercourses, in that they served as natural route guides (see chapter ten).

In the following three chapters, we examine an apparent need during the Neolithic to seek the sources of rivers. It appears that these were very 'special' places in the hill country of Britain. It is in these elevated locations that the majority of open-landscape British rock art is to be found, often close to spring lines and, frequently, in clusters. From these sites there are usually views down into river valleys or across distant flood plains, and in many cases there is a glimpse of the sea.

REFERENCES

Smith, B. A., and A. A. Walker, *Rock Art and Ritual: Interpreting the Prehistoric Landscapes of the North York Moors* (Stroud: Tempus, 2008).
Stout, G., and M. Stout, *Newgrange* (Cork University Press, 2008).

3

Basins

Within the upland regions of the present North York Moors are many 'basin' stones. Some of these were formed naturally, others have been modified, and some are manmade. Many have attracted additional carvings in the form of cups, or deliberately carved or modified grooves. These channels or grooves may lead into basins; others are overflow outlets for water, some linking with other basins. That basins were containers for water the authors have no doubt. A basin filled with rainwater in an elevated location was probably seen as water at its very purest, since it had come directly from the sky. Such water may have been endowed with special properties, akin perhaps to Christian holy water. We suggest in later chapters that basins, along with cup-and-ring motifs, may have been symbols for the birth of rivulets, streams and, eventually, rivers. This notion is developed further in chapters four, five and nine.

Natural processes may have formed the basin within a huge block of sandstone in Bransdale, North York Moors (illustrated in fig. 3). The channel leading in from above appears to have been enhanced by additional cutting. The short, straight 'outlet' definitely looks unnatural and artificially cut.

On Urra Moor, another massive block of sandstone has a large oval basin that is undercut and was therefore probably formed by the action of swirling water (fig. 4). At the bottom left of the above photograph is a short and very weathered inlet groove that looks artificial. In the Bransdale example it is the outlet groove that is short and straight. Neither could have been formed by water-flow. Were these cut as token gestures, as if inviting rainwater to fill a basin or to encourage flow from a basin? Also, the deeply cut outlet from the Cheddar Stone appears to have faint 'chiselling' at its base. Rock art researcher Paul Brown supplied us with a photograph taken in Nidderdale with a very similar short, straight inlet channel to a natural basin (fig. 5). A series of cups is also evident both within and beside the basin.

Returning to the North York Moors, another huge block of sandstone known as the Cheese Stone overlooks Baysdale to the north and has two sets of very rounded basins deeply cut into the top surface. Three basins at different levels flow water from the top basin down into the third. It then flows down a vertical surface of the stone via a series of V-shaped notches that appear to be artificially cut (fig. 6). Two further basins have exactly similar configurations.

Fig. 3. Basin, Bransdale, with inlet and outlet channels.

Fig. 4. The Cheddar Stone, showing basin and inlet/outlet.

Above: Fig. 5. Basin with short, deeply cut inlet groove and cups, Nidderdale. (*Paul Brown*)

Right: Fig. 6. Three linked basins, Cheese Stone.

Fig. 7. *Above:* The Beast Stone, with a glimpse of Roseberry. *Below:* Detail of miniature basin and 'V' outlet.

On the northern fringe of the Cleveland Hills, beneath the dramatic Wainstones outcrop, is another giant of a rock, sitting on the very edge of a steep escarpment at the mouth of Garfit Gap. On the top surface are irregular-shaped basins that are probably natural. Cups, some with rings, surround these. The basins themselves have channels in two separate areas; some parts of these outflow grooves show evidence of weathered artificial 'chiselling', presumably to improve water-flow between basins. Whether a stone or metal chisel or adze was used it is difficult to say, but would obviously have an important bearing on when these modifications were made, i.e. the Neolithic or the Early Bronze Age. Certainly the cups/cups-and-rings surrounding the basins and flow channels are very weathered and of soft appearance – typical of Neolithic rock art. A feature of this stone is the countersinking of cups, both within the basins and also at regular intervals within all of the flow channels (col. pl. 2). In the same field, another large block of sandstone has many of the features mentioned above. These two stones and their markings were therefore probably contemporaries (see chapter four).

Not all basins, or containers for water, are on the same massive scale as the examples mentioned above. On Battersby Moor, there are several large basins within earthfast rocks. There is also a stone here that might resemble some form of creature. Within the 'head' of this beast is a deeply hollowed basin. The outlet for water appears to be an artificially cut V-shaped notch (fig. 7).

Fig. 8. Linked cups and basins and flow channels, Brow Moor.

Artificially cut basins are to be found at several locations within the present North York Moors region. It is a matter of opinion as to when a cup becomes a basin. Perhaps a 10 cm diameter, or greater, might be a rough guide as to the size of a basin.

On Near Moor are three good examples that also have smaller cups within the same stone surface. These manmade basins do not have 'flow channels'. On Brow Moor, a large circular stone has both cups and basins deeply cut into the surface. Here there are limited flow channels, and some cups and basins have been deliberately linked (fig. 8).

Deep, smoothly rounded, artificial basins were probably formed by rotating a hard, rounded stone within an initial hollow within the surface of sandstone. An unusual discovery on the North York Moors referred to in our first volume of *Rock Art and Ritual* may provide the answer:

> On Ingleby Moor, between the Cheese Stone and Burton Howe (on Middle Head Top) is a huge block of sandstone beside a public footpath. This stone may hold the secret as to how deep rounded basins of the kind mentioned above were created. In 1998 a large, deep, rounded basin in this rock was observed to contain a stone with a circular flat top. When this heavy sandstone was lifted from the basin, the underside of the stone had clearly been ground smooth by rotation into a hemisphere that closely matched the 'negative' basin in which it was found resting. (Smith and Walker 2008, 131)

In chapter eleven, natural basins in granite tors on Bodmin Moor, Cornwall, are investigated by Alan. To date he has found no trace of artificial markings in association with them. However, he argues the case for a variety of Neolithic monuments being directly associated with tors containing basins. The phenomenon of basins is certainly not confined to Northern England. The possible reasons for their appeal to all prehistoric peoples are also discussed in chapter eleven.

REFERENCES

Brown, P., personal communication.
Smith, B. A., and A. A. Walker, *Rock Art and Ritual: Interpreting the Prehistoric Landscapes of the North York Moors* (Stroud: Tempus, 2008).

4

Frozen Flow

Fig. 9 was taken at Weetwood in Northumberland during heavy rain in 1997. It clearly illustrates the visual similarity of prehistoric rock motifs (cups with concentric rings) and the natural form of raindrops in water in the foreground (also see fig. 10). This observation may be purely coincidental, even fanciful, but the authors have explored the possible links between certain forms of rock-art and rainfall and water-flow over several years. The more we discover increases the probability that our initial hypothesis is viable. Our observations have largely been confined to Northern England, and the North York Moors in particular, but we have noted parallels in other parts of Britain and Ireland. Crucially, we also explore links with the Prehistoric Cosmos, at the interface of 'the three cosmic spheres' (Randsborg 1993, p. 113).

'WATER FEATURES' IN GARFIT GAP AND BEYOND

Beneath the spectacular natural rock-form of the Wainstones are two huge blocks of sandstone. One sits at the very shoulder of the Garfit Gap. Discovered in 2001, 'Rock 1' was seen to have weathered cups, some with rings, on the upper surface. In 2004, grass and debris were removed from hollows in the rock. When brushed clean, it was observed that channels, some artificially cut as if to create water-flow features, linked irregular hollows or 'basins'. All the basins had countersunk cups, and all the channels had cups at regular intervals along their courses. In the same field a second huge block of sandstone was found to have exactly similar features.

In the *Teesside Archaeological Society Bulletin* 12 (2007, 18), we stated:

Fascination with water and water-flow continues into the present day. Garden water-features have increased in popularity during recent years, if the expansion of areas within garden centres given over to plastic ponds of all shapes and dimensions is anything to go by. In prehistoric times, natural, modified, or manmade 'basins' containing water, apart from providing a small source of this precious commodity (although a spring does exist above the 'entrance' to Garfit Gap), may well have been endowed with qualities far beyond the utilitarian. As today, pure fascination with reflections and the flow of water may have been the sole inspiration for creating such features. At a time before glass and

Fig. 9. Rock art panel, Weetwood, Northumberland.

Fig. 10. Rainfall in a flooded garden border.

polished metal, however, reflections of the sky, clouds and heavenly bodies, and a glimpse of the person peering in, may have been a magical experience. Perhaps, for a brief while, a form of possession, even control over the sky, otherwise always and overwhelmingly above, may have seemed a reality. Glimpsing one's own face may have been a recognised way of communicating with the inner self. Watching rain fall from the sky above and, after contacting rocks, fill basins before flowing out along predetermined channels, ever downward, a microcosm of landscape, may also have been a form of imagined control. The creation of such water-features could, alternatively, have been a celebration of union between sky and the surface of the earth.

Eliade (1964, 259) has demonstrated that the sky and the land surface formed the two upper spheres of a tripartite Prehistoric Cosmos that he describes as the fundamental structure of a shamanic world-view, both past and present. Beneath the world of the living, with humans occupying the land surface, was the underworld, including the sea, which was 'the Realm of the Dead'. If this concept is accepted, links between sky and earth must have been seen as crucial to the continuation of life. Even if rejected, the same links would still have been seen as essential, but at the pragmatic level. Light and warmth and rain, essential in sustaining all life, originate in the sky. It is where contact is made with the land surface that the life-giving properties from the sky are transferred. It was perhaps seen as a kind of union. As suggested above, the celebration of such a union would explain an obsession with water features, and could also account for the apparent veneration of the Wainstones outcrop – reaching up as if to touch the sky.

Variations on the theme of 'water features' also occur at the eastern extreme of the North York Moors on Howdale Moor, above Robin Hood's Bay. One example is surrounded by water in prolonged inclement weather (see chapter eleven). Other examples are to be found at Allan Tofts (col. pl. 3). These 'kinetic' rock sculptures appear to have been created in order to control the flow of rainwater. Examples also occur at Lordenshaw and Old Bewick, Northumberland. Recently, examples of what appear to be long flow channels have been discovered in Patterdale, Cumbria, on huge slabs of sloping volcanic bedrock, along with numerous cups (Beckensall 2002).

Perhaps the sky–land interface was also seen as an event where rainwater was transferred at its very purest. Into existing clear water, raindrops form concentric rings of ripples. In all cases, the transfer appears to have been sufficiently important as to warrant the time and effort required in order to create such complex and fascinating features. Were such rock sculptures created in recognition of the life-sustaining properties of water? By making the image permanent in stone, were the carvers attempting to ensure the continuation of rainfall and its eventual flow into streams and rivers? As with the flow channels mentioned above, fig. 9 shows channels or grooves that appear to 'flow' from the cups at the centre of the concentric rings. Such linear grooves are frequently found in association with cups and rings. Invariably they progress down a slope or traverse a slope, often connecting with other linear grooves, reminiscent perhaps of the way that streams and rivers connect.

Above we considered the purity of a raindrop falling onto the land surface (or a pool of clear water). This could have been seen as leading directly to the birth of rivulets, streams and rivers that eventually die in the salt waters of the sea. The comparison with christening and 'born again' baptism ceremonies seems obvious – both employ pure water, or, in some instances, the immersion of the whole body in a river. If we are correct in deducing that the cup with rings is a representation of a raindrop falling into water and that this event was linked with the birth of a watercourse (fig. 9), this could mean that the cup with concentric rings is a **symbol of birth**. Also, the 'flow' channel from the centre cup might equally have been seen as the umbilical cord connecting the raindrop to a newborn stream.

Lewis-Williams and Pearce make a remarkably similar suggestion in *Inside the Neolithic Mind*. At the eastern entrance to the great Knowth passage tomb at the Brú na Bóinne is Circular Stone Setting No. 1:

> It is directly opposite the entrance to the tomb. Saucer-shaped, it is about 4.5 m (14.8 ft) from the entrance kerbstone, 4.2 m (13.8 ft) in diameter and was about 22 cm (8.7 in) below the old ground surface. It was scooped out of the ground. The interior of the setting was paved with small stones averaging about 15 by 10 cm (5.9 x 3.9 in). In the centre of the circle was a large square piece of grey limestone; it was firmly secured in the ground. Overlying the paving and the centre stone was a scatter of small quartz chips. The whole setting was surrounded by two rows of stones, one of which, the inner, was composed of glacial erratics; the outer row comprised clay ironstone nodules.
>
> … Then, at another level, the setting may have been an analogue of the carved stone basins in the eastern and western tombs. If so, was the symbolism of quartz related to that of water? To that question we add another: was there in the Neolithic mind a connection between a round pool, concentric, circular ripples widening from a dropped stone and nested circular and spiral motifs? Perhaps we can imagine a ritual at the eastern entrance to Knowth during which one or more pieces of quartz were tossed into the pool to create a water-constituted replica of carved motifs. (Lewis-Williams and Pearce 2005, 213–14)

In the fourth chapter of the first volume of *Rock Art and Ritual*, we noted that Eogan discovered a sandstone 'baetyl' lying on the old ground surface east of the entrance to Knowth 12, one of several smaller satellite tombs surrounding the great Knowth tomb. In that publication we argued that egg-shaped 'baetyls' were associated with the eastern sides of funerary monuments, and that they were symbols of the birth or rebirth of the soul – as per the 'reborn' sun rising each morning in the east. Lewis-Williams and Pearce reinforce our arguments. Bear in mind the birth symbolism that we believe is attached to concentric rings in open hill country, be they in water or carved in stone. As with 'baetyl' stones, it is uncanny that the circular setting No. 1 should be located at the east of a funerary monument.

THE SPIRAL – THE ANTITHESIS OF THE CUP?

The well-known spiral on the midwinter pillar of Long Meg is an anticlockwise one. So are two others recorded by Beckensall, one 90 cm above it, the other, almost eradicated, 35 cm from the ground at the south edge of the stone. This could be no more than coincidence, but Brennen did cite many other examples of the same occurrence: at Newgrange, at Barclodiad-y-Gawres, at Cape Clear in County Cork, at Knowth, and elsewhere. Long Meg, therefore, may possess one of the first megalithic symbols to be understood in modern times. (Burl, 1999, 40–1)

We also cite Burl's *The Stone Circles of the British Isles* (Burl 1976, 141):

Once beyond Crinan a traveller found himself once more in Atlantic waters. Here the leather-sided and shallow-drafted vessels would be paddled between the islands and the mainland. Earlier tragedies warned seafarers to avoid the fatal Gulf of Corryvreckan between the islands of Jura and Scarba where the narrow channels create irresistible races. 'Any small craft … that is swept there by the flood (and there is no turning back) against the seas raised by a westerly gale, has little chance of survival in the terrific seas that break from the whirlpool for several miles to the west.' (Thom 1971, 10)

Whirlpools are terrifying swirling vortices, and there are several off the western coast of Scotland. The Neolithic seafarers would have lived in dread of being drawn into the sea's equivalent of a black hole. Although these sailors regularly used the sea from the Atlantic coast of Europe (Bradley 1997), 'to the Outer Hebrides and ultimately the Orkneys' (Burl 1976, 141), their cosmological belief system recognised the sea as being the Realm of the Dead. Together with the underworld beneath the land's surface, this realm constituted the lower part of a tripartite Prehistoric Cosmos (Eliade 1964, 259).

Is it possible that the whirlpool vortex was given graphic form as a spiral? Could this motif be a terrible anticlockwise symbol for entry into the Realm of the Dead? The line to Long Meg from the centre of her circle points to the midwinter sunset, an event associated with death. The midwinter sunrise illuminates the passage grave of Newgrange, where again we find anticlockwise spirals at the entrance (fig. 11). Was this huge monument built to symbolise a journey into the underworld? A decorated basin is the focal point in the Newgrange chamber. Did this hold water? Stan Beckensall hints at comparisons with the church font bowl and the concept of 'being born again' (Beckensall 2006, 112).

The spiral is a rare motif in known open-air contexts. As noted above, three are present on Long Meg. A double-linked example can be seen at the Temple Wood stone circle in Argyll. Further north, on Orkney, are several examples originally associated with chambered tombs. Others at entrances to (and within) passage graves occur on Anglesey: Barclodiad y Gawres and Bryn Celli Ddu are good examples. All the spiral motifs have been carved into the vertical surfaces of stones, and all of these ritual monuments are geographically located in the west of Britain, where contact with Ireland would have been probable (with the exception of Orkney in the far north). On the entrance stone of the passage grave 'Stoney Littleton' in Somerset is the fossil impression of a huge ammonite, a naturally occurring spiral. The Neolithic was a period of extensive sea travel (see chapter one), and the spiral motif of the passage graves could easily have been taken to new shores by these adventurers.

Fig. 11. Newgrange entrance.

Strangely, two river cliffs in the extreme east of Britain, one on the banks of the River North Esk in Lothian, Scotland, and the other above the River Coquet in Northumberland, have spirals on vertical surfaces. Unlike the examples given above, these motifs are *not* associated with ritual monuments, but we believe we understand the reason for their 'natural' location. This will be discussed in some detail in later chapters.

It is clear that the spiral was a powerful symbol. We conclude chapter four with the fact that the spiral 'can also signify a path or passageway to the spiritual world' (Ripinsky-Naxon 1993, 112). It is associated with the process of entering a state of trance (Pearson 2002). Based upon the spatial distribution of spirals (singly, apparently all anticlockwise) within and in association with Irish passage graves, Dronfield (1996) has argued convincingly that these motifs represent passages to, or points of access with, other worlds. In ecstatic states of trance, contact with the ancestors was possible through these passages, and the souls of the recent dead could pass safely to the ancestral realm.

REFERENCES

Beckensall, S., col. pl. 4 in *Prehistoric Rock Art in Cumbria: Landscapes and Monuments* (Stroud: Tempus, 2002).

Beckensall, S., *Circles in Stone: A British Prehistoric Mystery* (Stroud: Tempus, 2006).

Bradley, R., chap. 2 in *Rock Art and the Prehistory of Atlantic Europe* (London: Routledge, 1997).

Burl, A., *The Stone Circles of the British Isles* (Yale University Press, 1976).

Burl, A., *Great Stone Circles* (Yale University Press, 1999).

Dronfield, J., 'Entering Alternative Realities: Cognition, Art and Architecture in Irish Passage Tombs' in *Cambridge Archaeological Journal* 6.1, pp. 37–72 (1996).

Eliade, M., *Shamanism, Archaic Techniques of Ecstasy* (London: Penguin, 1964).

Lewis-Williams, D., and D. Pearce, *Inside the Neolithic Mind* (London: Thames & Hudson, 2005).

Pearson, J. L., *Shamanism and the Ancient Mind: A Cognitive Approach to Archaeology* (Walnut Creek CA: Altamira Press, 2002).

Randsborg, K., 'Kivik: Archaeology and Iconography' in *Acta Archaeologica Academiae Scientarum* 64.1, pp. 1–147 (1993).

Ripinsky-Naxon, M., *The Nature of Shamanism: Substance and Function of a Religious Metaphor* (Albany: State University of New York Press, 1993).

Smith, B. A., and A. A. Walker, 'The Wainstones: Prehistoric Link between Sky and Earth
 – Monumental Rock Art Below' in *Teesside Archaeological Society Bulletin* 12, p. 18 (2007).
Smith, B. A., and A. A. Walker, col. pl. 13c–f in *Rock Art and Ritual: Interpreting the Prehistoric Landscapes of the North York Moors* (Stroud: Tempus, 2008).

5

Old Man River

In chapters one and two, we looked at the practicalities of using the sea and rivers as a means of travel by boat during the Neolithic. Both Neolithic humans and the Norse Vikings perhaps 4,000 years later inhabited the Atlantic-facing mainland of Europe and the islands to the west and north. They were seagoing adventurers of great daring. In both cases, access to the interior of landmasses was, from their seagoing perspective, usually by travelling upstream from a river mouth as far as was navigable. If we were able to meet such people today, there surely could be nothing that we could tell them about water and its 'behaviour' and characteristics. From the comparative safety of our modern vessels, with their built-in echo-sounding devices, satellite-navigation systems and powerful engines, seafarers today are, to some extent, detached from the nature of the watery medium on which they travel.

Neolithic people, by contrast, would have been only too aware of races, tides, swirls, eddies, waves and currents affecting both sea and river. Such must have been the turbulent nature of their direct experiences that, safely on shore, or riverbank, the enormity of a safe passage may have led to a culture that revered water, and water-flow, and sought some kind of thanksgiving for a safe return. Did they create artworks in stone, often of great beauty, that appear to exalt and express water-flow in order to ensure safe passage in the future? Like everything during the Neolithic, this may have been one part of the reason for such exotic carvings.

Even 5,000–6,000 years ago, rivers would have appeared to be eternal, ever-flowing, and as old as the hills. To a culture that lived with the spirits of their ancestors, respect and even veneration of rivers was a strong possibility. Some of the oldest place names in Britain and Ireland, with origins going back to at least the Celts, are those of rivers. The meanings of such names, in North East England, are descriptive, even poetic:

> Don – *water*
> Kielder – *violent stream*
> Leven – *smooth*
> Lyne – *flowing*
> Ouse – *surging, bubbling*
> Tees – *surging*
> Tweed – *swelling, powerful*
> Tyne – *flow*
> Wear – *water, river* (Robinson 1999, 110)

In this chapter, we consider a (reversed) source-to-sea veneration of water and of water-flow that ties in with the Prehistoric Cosmos and explains the location and nature of numerous examples of Neolithic rock art in the open landscape, as well as funerary monuments.

As they penetrated further inland, beyond navigable rivers and streams, the Neolithic people may have sought the sources of their rivers – special places, perhaps of spiritual importance, in the hills above the river valleys. Certainly the majority of open-air rock art is located in such places, and looks down into river valleys in Ireland and Britain. It begins to appear that the rivers themselves were in some way sacred to the Neolithic belief system, and that they had a beginning and an end – in other words, rivers possessed a kind of life. Indeed, it becomes increasingly probable in our investigations that **rivers were metaphors for the flow of life**.

Earlier (in chapter four) we suggested that the purity of a raindrop falling from the upper layer of their cosmos, the sky, and contacting the earth's surface, the habitable layer of the cosmos, could have been seen as an event whereby life-giving properties were transferred. Such raindrops would have created concentric rings of ripples in basins, ponds, lakes and rivers. In still conditions, the effect would have been most noticeable in the first three locations, which are also places where reflections – reversed images of the world around and the sky above – occur. This may well have been a magical visual experience at a time before glass or metal mirrors. Such imagery, of raindrops into water in particular, may have led to the creation of cup and concentric ring motifs carved into stone. Such motifs were not only symbols for the birth of a river, but symbols for birth itself.

Similarly, basins themselves (as we argued in chapters five and nine of our first volume) were probably symbolically linked with birth, especially in elevated hill locations. They may equally have been associated with death and rebirth. The latter connection is almost certainly true where basins are located within such passage tombs in Ireland as Knowth and Newgrange. The example cited at the east entrance to Knowth in chapter four could be classed as a basin, and if Lewis-Williams and Pearce are correct in proposing that quartz pieces were thrown into the water contained within, in order to create concentric circular ripples, the connection is all too clear. Both basin and concentric rings would have been brought together in one powerful symbolic event.

Let us return to hill country. On a number of rocks, particularly in Northumberland, such motifs, in combination with deep grooves and the natural surface undulations of the rock, take the notion of water being a living, flowing, turbulent entity into the realms of kinetic sculpture. Indeed, it seems as though their creators were attempting to transform these rocks into water itself, as they would have observed it in rivers or in the sea. Fabulous examples are located in Northumberland, at Lordenshaw and Old Bewick. These rocks appear to be freezing flow, as if turned into fossil rivers – they were three-dimensional snapshots in stone. Surely, through such sculptures, the Neolithic people were paying homage to water and to rivers (col. pl. 4, 5, 12).

A small area of the massive Roughting Linn ('roaring water') rock is illustrated (col. pl. 6). The carvings are in deep relief, despite perhaps 5,000 years having passed since their creation in the Neolithic. Virtually all of the motifs on this huge 'whale-back' of

Fig. 12. Roughting Linn, two channels on the west slope.

Fig. 13. Rock carved 'tunnel'.

a rock are on sloping surfaces. Linear grooves, whether leading from cups or cup-and-rings, or from natural sources, strongly suggest that these were artificially engraved 'flow channels', associated with water and with the control of water-flow. Indeed, the entire rock may have been visualised during the Neolithic as a hill in miniature, with motifs deeply engraved, probably as symbols of birth and the 'flow of life'. On the western slope of this rock are two long channels running from top to bottom. These cut through the natural grain or layers of the rock and are therefore artificial. Again, these appear to have only one purpose – water-flow (fig. 12). On a much smaller scale, compare Roughting Linn with the deep flow channels on the Allan Tofts rocks, North York Moors, discussed in chapter four (col. pl. 3).

Stranger still, on the east slope of Roughting Linn, a short 'tunnel' appears to have been artificially sculpted, presumably to allow water to flow *beneath* the rock surface from a deep channel above (fig. 13).

Two rock art sites mentioned earlier, also in Northumberland hill country, at Lordenshaw and Old Bewick, have examples that are different from Roughting Linn. Their difference lies in the fact that these early artists have transformed huge rocks as if into turbulent, swirling rivers. They were not simply applying symbolic motifs to 'decorate' a rock surface that may have been emulating a hill; these are rock sculptures, capable of holding their own in any modern sculpture park or gallery. Apparently abstract at first sight, these amazing rock sculptures must surely be representations of rivers in full flow, coming to life especially during rainfall and under certain lighting conditions (col. pl. 4, 12).

Humbler rock carvings on the North York Moors seem to be telling the same story (see chapter eleven). Further examples are to be found in Cumbria (Beckensall 2002). All are situated in hill country where rivers are 'born' and where there is rarely a shortage of rainfall.

Hill streams become the tributaries of rivers occupying the valley bottoms, forever flowing towards their 'old age' stage as they meander over low-level flood plains and finally 'die' in the salt waters of the sea. It is at these 'old age' stages that a different form of rock art is to be found, usually in association with Neolithic funerary monuments. Other sites directly overlook the sea – the inevitable destination of rivers – which is associated with the Realm of the Dead in the Prehistoric Cosmos.

(Sites mentioned in this chapter have also been referred to in chapters four and eight. With regard to rock art beside the 'old age' stage of rivers, or overlooking the sea, and its association with funerary monuments or rare open-landscape locations, please refer to chapter nine, where a focused appraisal has been made.)

It is relevant here to refer to a major recent discovery, described (under the title 'Newhenge') as Bluestonehenge in an article published in *British Archaeology* 110 (Parker Pearson, Pollard, Thomas and Welham 2009, 14–21).

In 2008, stoneholes were excavated that formed part of a 10 m-diameter circle. These were believed to have held bluestone monoliths. This stone circle had been situated within a henge earthwork on the banks of the River Avon, at the beginning of the 'Avenue' that leads uphill to the north-east entrance of Stonehenge. Dating evidence suggests that this henge and circle predated Stonehenge, and that the bluestones may have been re-used in the rebuild of Stonehenge itself.

Although incomplete, excavation within the recently discovered henge has revealed a large quantity of charcoal on the old ground surface, including a fragment of human bone. Dating from as far back as 5,000 BP, this structure is clearly of Neolithic origin, with evidence of reuse well into the Bronze Age. Cremation and funerary rituals here were in direct association with a river. In chapters eight and nine such an association is re-emphasised during the Neolithic period, both within Britain and Ireland. Much further afield (and still practised today), cremation ceremonies are an everyday occurrence beside the rivers Ganges and Bagmati in India and Nepal. Ancient Egyptian funerary ritual was linked with the River Nile (see chapter twelve).

REFERENCES

Beckensall, S., *Prehistoric Rock Art in Cumbria: Landscapes and Monuments* (Stroud: Tempus, 2002).

Parker Pearson, M., J. Pollard, J. Thomas, and K. Welham, 'Newhenge' in *British Archaeology* 110, pp. 14–21 (York: CBA, 2010).

Robinson, I., *From Abberwick to Yetlington: The Place-Names of North-East England* (Durham: GP Electronic Services, 1999).

Conclusion to Part One

Although there can be little doubt that rainfall, water and water-flow were of fundamental importance with regard to the shaping and forming of certain kinds of open landscape rock art during the Neolithic period, there are regional variations. This might suggest that some were created outside a possible mainstream of rock art development.

In chapter four, the classic cup with concentric rings is considered and we find that long grooves or channels frequently run down-slope from the central cups of these motifs. We are convinced that such channels were created for water-flow and that, in combination with cup and ring motifs, they may have been a symbol for the birth of a stream, and indeed for birth in general. Cup and ring motifs with flow channels from central cups are to be found along the eastern side of the Pennine watershed, in Northumberland, south-west Scotland and in Argyll. By far the most numerous and spectacular examples are to be found in Northumberland and Argyll. However, this combination is *not* true of the open-landscape rock art of either Cumbria or the North York Moors.

Known open-landscape rock art in Cumbria and the North York Moors frequently has 'flow' channels, but these do not emanate from the centre of cup-and-ring motifs. Within these two regions, flow channels may run from or into cups or basins (be they manmade or natural), or simply from the top of a rock. Cups, sometimes within the basins and channels themselves, often accompany such 'flow' channels. It is not that cup-and-ring motifs do not exist in these two regions; indeed, within the Fylingdales Moors, above Robin Hood's Bay on the North Sea coast, there are six such motifs with short 'gutters' linking the central cup to beyond the outer ring. These short grooves are not 'flow' channels, however; they do not run down-slope. Because of their easterly or southerly orientations, we suggest that their target was sunrise or the midday sun (see chapters eight and nine).

Were Cumbria and the North York Moors in some way detached from the mainstream of the stylistic development of rock motifs that was so consistent within the huge expanse of the regions mentioned above? The inhabitants of Cumbria and the North York Moors also apparently revered water, and water-flow in particular. In common with the other regions, they shared such rock art features as basins, cups and flow channels, but the link between cup-and-ring motifs and flow channels emanating from the central cup is blatantly missing. Nevertheless, in relation to water and to water-flow, all of the regions were speaking a similar language.

Was some form of isolation – temporal, geographical or even political – responsible for variations being developed on the same theme? Is it also possible that rock art water features were *initially* created within Cumbria or the North York Moors, and that these led to sophisticated developments elsewhere? Or were these two regions 'backwaters' as regards developments in rock art?

PART TWO

OF RAYS AND THE SUN

Introduction to Part Two

Seen separately, or in combination with water-flow, energy from the sun (be it light or heat) must have been as important to the Neolithic and Early Bronze Age inhabitants of these islands as water. Both were essential to life.

Evidence for the veneration of the sun and sunlight is to be found in built monuments such as stone circles and passage tombs, as well as in certain kinds of rock motifs. Their location within the landscape and their relation to the angle of sunlight was as important as the nature of these monumental structures and the rock carvings themselves. Indeed, it appears that all of these elements had been considered together as a complete design package, often for calendrical or cosmological purposes.

Variations on the same theme are to be found throughout the British Isles. Throughout history, the construction of monuments and the creation of rock art directly relating to the sun must be seen as a global phenomenon (col. pl. 7).

6

Reaching for the Sky

In 2003, during a visit to Castlerigg Stone Circle – possibly *the* most romantic of all circle settings, surrounded as it is by dramatically beautiful Cumbrian Mountains – Brian noticed an interesting phenomenon. The shape of the tops of several standing stones appeared to be an almost exact match for those of mountains beyond. Two such examples are shown opposite (fig. 14). Of course, such an association could be purely coincidental; nevertheless the idea is appealing. The Neolithic and Bronze Age people certainly had a highly developed sense of shape and form, as can be seen in their stone tools, for example. The Cumbrian greenstone axes were shaped and finished to become objects of great beauty, far beyond what was necessary for their mundane use as a tool. The same is true of their finely flaked flint arrowheads, the result of many hours of careful crafting, whereas a pointed flint with minimal work could have been used for killing nearly as effectively. Considering the number of arrows that must have been lost, or damaged, it becomes more than probable that finely worked arrowheads and stone axes were elevated into the realm of status objects: they must also have been used as gifts, funerary objects, or in exchange as a form of currency. Of course, many examples of Neolithic rock art, the central issue of this volume, can be incredibly visually exciting, especially under certain light or surface water conditions. These people were high-calibre artists and craftsmen in every sense.

Returning to the possible visual link between the Castlerigg stones and the summits of mountains beyond, there could also be a connection with the Cumbrian stone-axe quarries high in the Langdale Pikes. In their book *Interpreting the Axe Trade*, Richard Bradley and Mark Edmonds make the following observation based on intensive fieldwork at Langdale Pikes:

> Here we find both quarries and open-cast workings, yet many of the areas with suitable raw material do not seem to have been used at all. Although there is considerable evidence of stone extraction at Top Buttress, parts of the same outcrop between Middle/East Gully and Loft Crag do not appear to have been exploited. This is particularly surprising, considering that many of these unused areas are easier to reach than Top Buttress itself, raising the intriguing possibility that the choice of extraction site was determined by factors other than topography and geology. (Bradley and Edmonds 2005, 102)

Fig. 14. Two Castlerigg Circle stones apparently shape-matching mountains beyond.

Tying in with our suggestion that stone axes were more than just tools, many examples of axeheads from Cumbrian sources, used, reshaped and *unused*, have been discovered throughout the length and breadth of England and in parts of Scotland (Bradley and Edmonds 2005, fig. 3.1). *Interpreting the Axe Trade* also notes that axes from distant sources occur where local stone was been quarried for exactly the same purpose. This seems to imply that the intrinsic value of such an object was partly dependent on its distant source and a sense of mystique, and perhaps even its magical properties. Further value might have been recognised in the knowledge that objects of such great beauty came from seams of stone within the very highest mountains of Cumbria. Here, not only was difficulty and danger a part of the stone extraction process, the materials also came from a source that was as close as possible to the sky itself.

LOOKING AND SEEING

Many visitors come to look and marvel at Castlerigg, an ancient circle set within the mountains of Cumbria. Few, however, will actually *see* anything.

There are many ways of seeing. Sunlight enables us to look with our eyes. But it is the connections made in the mind's eye, the moments of realisation, that give us the ability to really *see* something.

Perhaps a visual artist within the circle would experience the 'shape-matching' of standing stones with mountains beyond (as was described above). This may lead to a further realisation: perhaps Castlerigg was a kind of replica, a ring set within a ring, and linked by certain stones that appear to replicate and thereby connect with the encircling mountains.

The late Professor Alexander Thom visited Castlerigg as part of his lifelong study of stone circles (and standing stones in general) throughout the British Isles and beyond. With the eye of a surveyor, Thom was concerned with measurement, geometry, calculation and alignments. His high-precision methods of working enabled him to *see* alignments from this circle without the need to actually experience them. For Castlerigg these included the midsummer setting sun, the midwinter sunrise, and various lunar alignments (Wood 1978, 95).

A romantic poet such as the Lake District's Wordsworth probably preferred misty and mysterious atmospheric effects as his way of *seeing* ancient standing stones, as if the world was a kind of theatre filled with stage-sets.

Recent rock art researchers might largely ignore any relationship that the circle may have had with the world around and concentrate on examining the surfaces of stones in order to identify motifs. Later, in chapter eight, there is an example, within this very circle, of a spiral that researchers were unable to see with their eyes, yet they were able to make rubbings in order to establish its existence.

A philosopher may have recognised the symbolism of a ring within a ring, not in the artist's visual terms, but as a representation of the mind's eye looking outwards in order to connect with the world around it.

A well-known metaphor for realisation and understanding is 'seeing the light'. Even the mind's eye cannot function entirely on its own. It requires cues from the world of light outside the self. In the process of looking and seeing, the sun and sunlight remain of paramount importance. Prehistoric people throughout the world have often gone to extreme lengths in order to demonstrate their allegiance to that bright disc in the sky. Some cultures actually saw the sun as a deity; to others it was a vital part of existence and a key component within their cosmos.

CONNECTIONS

Half a world away, in the high Andes of South America, the Incas built their enigmatic 'Lost City' of Machu Picchu. Discovered in 1911 by Hiram Bingham, this marvel of Inca stonework still holds many secrets. Without doubt the Incas were a culture that worshipped the sun, and their rulers were seen as direct descendants of the sun, as implied by the Temple of the Sun in Cuzco, the Inca capital until Spain's bloody conquest and quest for gold in the sixteenth century. It is probable that Machu Picchu was an ancient retreat of Inca rulers long before the Spanish arrived. It must have taken many years (probably hundreds of years) of hard work, using the best masons, to construct such a complex hundreds of metres above the nearest valley floor. This included the construction of high terracing along the sides of mountains in order to grow crops to sustain such a 'royal' or religious complex. The tenacity of the Inca people certainly equals the building programmes directed by the pharaohs in their building of pyramids beside the River Nile. Interestingly, both of these cultures worshipped the sun as an actual deity.

The Temple of the Sun in Cuzco (built over by the Spanish with a Christian church in order to eradicate pagan sun worship) was replicated at Machu Picchu. A similar semicircular tower appears to 'grow' out of the rock; it was constructed of the finest granite masonry. Also at Machu Picchu, a stone staircase climbs a small hill to the major shrine, the Intihuatana. This Quechua word loosely translates as 'the hitching post of the sun' and refers to a carved rock pillar that stands on the top of the hill. The whole complex lies beneath a huge tapering pillar of rock that may have been seen as a 'natural Intihuatana' and was perhaps the initial inspiration for the choice of site.

Recent investigations at Machu Picchu have revealed 'shape-matching' links with surrounding high mountain peaks. Hard granite stones within the complex had apparently been shaped to echo the forms of these mountains. If true, such stones must represent countless hours of hard and careful chipping and fine grinding.

Surely there can be no direct connection between the apparent shape-matching of stones within a Lake District stone circle and its surrounding fell summits, and similar phenomena thousands of miles away (and thousands of years later) in the high Andes of Peru? Could it be, then, that the desire to connect with the highest mountains, and reach as close as possible towards the sky in order to link with the heavens, and the sun in particular, is hard-wired into the human brain?

Another culture in South America that was destroyed by Spanish soldiers and the friars who came with them was that of the Maya. On the Yucatán Peninsula in Mexico the stunning ruins of their cities and ceremonial sites can still be seen, many reclaimed from the jungle. Like the Incas, the Mayan civilisation worshipped the sun as a deity they called Kinich Ahau. They also had other gods such as Chac, the rain god, and the staring-eyed Tialoc, god of rain and lightning. Mictlantecuhtli was god of their underworld. Unlike the Incas, who lived in the high Andes, the Yucatán Peninsula lacked mountains. In order to reach for the sky, these people apparently built their own, in the form of gigantic stepped pyramids (col. pl. 8). The Ancient Egyptians, who worshipped the sun as a god, Re, also recognised other deities. Like the Maya, they built pyramids that reached into the sky from the flat plain beside the River Nile.

In Britain we also have a manmade hill, the highest in Europe, rising from the rolling downs of Wiltshire, an area also lacking significant hills or mountains. In *The Stone Circles of the British Isles*, Aubrey Burl gives the height of Silbury Hill as 39.5 metres. Citing Atkinson, Burl then gives the following calculation:

> As Silbury Hill took about 18,000,000 man-hours to complete it can be reckoned that even with 500 labourers working through each autumn the project would have endured for well over fifty years, probably longer. Even with a year-long labour-force the earthwork would have taken fifteen years to build. (Cited in Burl 1976, 327)

Unlike the pyramids in Mexico and Egypt, Silbury Hill was constructed of earth instead of stone; the few stones found on the Wiltshire Downs were used to build the nearby circles of Avebury and Stonehenge. During limited excavation on the summit, Fachtna

Fig. 15. The Rudstone Monolith.

McAvoy of English Heritage found a fragment of antler from a secure context. This produced a secure radiocarbon date of 2490–2340 BC, placing the mound firmly in the Late Neolithic (*British Archaeology* 70, 16). This artificial hill is therefore as ancient as the Old Kingdom pyramids of Egypt, and certainly far older than the monuments in Mexico and Peru. Also, Silbury does not appear to be a burial mound.

If at least part of the purpose of the above structures was to reach into the sky, the huge, tapering standing stones in North Yorkshire may well have been brought from many miles away and erected near Boroughbridge, and on the Yorkshire Wolds at Rudston, for the same purpose. These are the impressive Devil's Arrows and the Rudston Monolith, at some 7.7 metres high the tallest monolith in Britain, even though the top is missing (fig. 15).

In our immediate history, we have experienced not only the first man on the Moon, but also a still-continuing exploration of the planets within our solar system, as relayed back to Earth and into our living rooms. The advances in technology have been incredible and our goals are ever more challenging as a result. The human desire to 'reach for the sky' has certainly not diminished since our ancestors attempted to connect with the heavens and heavenly bodies, even though our reasons for doing so have fundamentally altered.

REFERENCES

Atkinson, R. J. C., 'Ancient Astronomy: Unwritten Evidence' in *The Place of Astronomy in the Ancient World*, ed. F. R. Hodson (London: Oxford University Press, 1974).

Bradley, R., and M. Edmonds, *Interpreting the Axe Trade: Production and Exchange in Neolithic Britain* (Cambridge University Press, 2005).

Burl, A., *The Stone Circles of the British Isles* (London: Yale University Press, 1979).

Inman, N., *Mexico* (London: Dorling Kindersley, 2006).

McAvoy, F., in *British Archaeology* 70 (York: CBA, 2003).

Rachowiecki, R., *Peru* (China: Lonely Planet, 2004).

Wood, J. E., *Sun, Moon and Standing Stones* (Oxford University Press, 1978).

7

Aligning with the Sun

The photographs opposite (fig. 16) show standing stones within two early Cumbrian stone circles. On the left is a north–south alignment at the Castlerigg Circle that runs past the inner edge of a north entrance portal, skims the side of a portal stone at the south of the circle, and aligns with a mountain crag beyond. The right-hand photograph shows that the south stone at Swinside is far more bulky than the slim, tapering north stone and may have been chosen for its eye-catching layered quartz intrusions. Was it positioned to shape-match the top of a nearby fell?

Establishing north and south would have been of paramount importance to the Neolithic people who constructed these early circles. In part one we presented a case for early Neolithic people being great sea adventurers, akin to the Vikings 4,000 years later. In order to navigate, it must have been an essential prerequisite that they were capable, at the very least, of determining the cardinal directions of north and south. Today, of course, we can use a compass or GPS in order to establish such directionality. During the Neolithic, finding north greatly depended on the sun's position in the sky. They would have known that when it was highest in the sky, the sun was directly south. They would also have known that the sun does not enter the north of the sky.

Referring to the Cumbrian Long Meg Circle, Aubrey Burl makes the following comments about cardinal points within the structure of stone circles:

Like several other great Cumbrian rings Long Meg contained not only a calendrical line but one to a cardinal point. At Castlerigg and Swinside it was the north, at Mayburgh the east, at Long Meg the west. Unlike the calendrical settings these cardinal lines are rarely accurate to more than a degree or two. The writer believes that circle-builders were concerned not with the abstract concept of a cardinal position but with the point midway between two solar extremes, at Long Meg presumably that between the midwinter and midsummer settings. Had the western skyline been level this would have been at True West, 270°. The horizon at Long Meg, however, was nearly a degree higher to the south-west causing the sun to disappear below the horizon sooner. This 'pulled' the midpoint a little to the south so that the gigantic western boulder stood not at 270° but at 267°, equidistant between the observed winter and summer settings. What looks like cardinal inaccuracy to today's investigator was solar precision to the people who set up the stone. (Burl 1999, 42)

NORTH

Fig. 16. Two north-south stone
alignments. *Above:* Castlerigg
Circle. *Right:* Swinside Circle.

Fig. 17. A garden experiment.

A TWENTY-FIRST-CENTURY EXPERIMENT

Knowing that the sun, when due south, is at its highest point in the sky, it logically follows that a shadow cast by the sun, when at its shortest, would point directly north. With the advantage of having a watch, this would occur at around 1 p.m. British Summer Time (and adjusted to local time) in June, actually midday without the timeshift. A gnomon comprising of a dowel, with a Neolithic flint arrowhead inserted, and set into a block of wood was placed on a perfectly horizontal paving stone and a chalk line drawn around, should it be accidentally disturbed. Of course, any vertical pointed shaft would have sufficed. It just seemed more authentic to replicate an arrow. Indeed, such a choice for a gnomon may well have been used during the Neolithic or the Early Bronze Age.

The experiment began around 8.30 a.m. BST on a cloudless summer's morning; the weather forecast was for unbroken sunshine. Approximately every 10 minutes, the shadow cast by the tip of the gnomon was marked with a chalk dot. As the morning progressed, it became clear that the arrowhead was scribing a curved line. It also became clear that a shadow cast by a nearby tree was going to curtail proceedings at around 1.30 p.m. The shadow *was* at its shortest at midday, after which it gradually started lengthening again. A chalk line was drawn from the base of the gnomon through the shortest shadow length. This was a true north–south line. In the photograph taken at the end of the experiment (fig. 17), it can be seen that the block into which the dowel was inserted was not initially set square to the north–south line that eventually emerged. This makes it appear that the chalked curve was nearer the gnomon at around 12.30. Ideally, the dowel should have been directly fixed to the paving stone, but would have required drilling into it.

This method of establishing a true north–south line could easily have been achieved during the Neolithic period and in the Bronze Age. It is also clear that, as a consequence, they could have created a basic sundial that indicated midday at any time of the year (providing that the sun was shining). Furthermore, by marking the lengths of shadows along the north–south line throughout the year, they could have established a sun calendar. The very shortest shadow would have been cast at midsummer, and the longest at midwinter. Sub-divisions would have further divided the year, although we know that the lunar months were almost certainly recorded by six- and twelve-cup 'domino' stones, probably during the Neolithic and into the Early Bronze Age (see chapter nine).

The taller the gnomon, the more accurate such a method would have been. Tall, tapering standing stones would have been ideal and permanent. The latter point would have been essential should daily use as a sundial, or use throughout the year as a sun calendar, have been envisaged. In chapter six we mentioned the Devil's Arrows and the Rudstone Monolith, both in North Yorkshire (fig. 15). Such stones would have been eminently suitable, and all have been deliberately tapered – no light task without metal tools. Unfortunately, ground disturbance over thousands of years would have eliminated any evidence of their use as gnomons for sun clocks or calendars. A prerequisite of this suggestion would have been a large, smooth, flat area of ground. The sun would need to have been shining strongly.

BROW MOOR'S ASTRO-GEOMETRIC ZONE

The photograph overleaf (fig. 18), taken in evening sunlight at midsummer, clearly shows a pecked cross on a flat, gently sloping stone surface. We are in an elevated area on Brow Moor (above Ravenscar on the North York Moors), which we dubbed the Astro-Geometric Zone after discovering stones with motifs that appear to have been imposed on their surfaces. These were uncompromisingly deliberate, clearly pecked and essentially linear and geometric, quite unlike the majority of motifs on stones in the open landscape that probably belong to the Neolithic (although they are weathered, peckmarks are still evident on these stones; they probably belong to the more recent Early Bronze Age). Furthermore, the Cross Stone, and others nearby in the Astro-Geometric Zone, had been precisely aligned to either cardinal points, or to key sunset events on a distant (and incredibly level) western skyline.

The arms of the Cross Stone, although they deviate in length, are accurately aligned to the north–south and east–west cardinal points. Close examination of the south-orientated arm shows a neat line of fine dots pecked into the surface alongside it. This

Fig. 18. The Astro-Geometric Zone Cross Stone.

may well have been the original north–south line that was later revised, even though only by a degree or two. If so, this means that accuracy in the layout of cardinals was seen as being very important in this example (fig. 19).

Another interesting feature of the Cross Stone is the location of single cups in three of the quadrants between the arms of the cross. Views of distant skylines to the south-west, north-west and north-east correspond with the quadrants containing cups. In the south-east quadrant, which has no cup, the view is blocked by a nearby rise in the moor. As with the earlier example given of the Castlerigg Circle, this does seem to suggest a need to link with the surrounding landscape (also see chapter six). The difference with Castlerigg, believed by Burl to be 'one of the earliest circles in Europe, its stones raised around 3200 BC' (Burl 1995, 43), is that that we believe the Cross Stone, and others in the Astro-Geometric Zone, belong to the Early Bronze Age. If we are correct, this means a continuation of elements of a Neolithic belief system (including the use of stone circles) into the Early Bronze Age.

Nearby, in Brow Moor's Astro-Geometric Zone, is the 'RAF' Stone (see also chapter eight) with east–west aligned cups and concentric rings. These motifs are very weathered and appear to belong to the Neolithic tradition of spatial sensitivity in their placement at either end of a naturally east–west orientated, earthfast rock. Between these two motifs, a linear groove, still clearly showing peckmarks (and similar weathering to the Cross Stone above), is closely aligned to the north–south cardinals. Again, this example seems to demonstrate that the activities of a later Early Bronze Age culture retained links with a Neolithic past (fig. 20).

Above: Fig. 19. The Cross Stone.

Right: Fig. 20. The RAF Stone and an autumn equinoctial sunset.

THE HUGH KENDALL STONE

In our first volume, the connection was made between the open-landscape Hugh Kendall Stone (named after its discoverer in 1937) and a cairn, currently visible from the Astro-Geometric Zone, both on Brow Moor. In 2004, a 10 per cent excavation of this cairn caused a national stir in the world of archaeology (and among rock art specialists in particular) by exposing a slab of stone with extraordinary markings on its surface. Scant attention was given to the structural layout of the cairn itself. We now believe that the pictogram on the earthfast stone and the plan of the cairn share crucial orientations. These not only relate to the surrounding landscape, but also display calendrical knowledge based on solar observation. Elements of the Prehistoric Cosmos also appear to be encoded within both designs.

The Hugh Kendall Stone has a deeply pecked line running south-west–north-east, from edge to edge towards the western end. An irregular arc has been pecked from close to the south-west end of the line, rising gradually then dropping steeply to the approximate mid-point of the line. At the very crest of this arc is a cup-and-ring motif. A single cup lies to the east of the south-west–north-east line, immediately below the cup-and-ring motif (fig. 21).

If we consider the view from this stone towards the west, we see a distant skyline, remarkably level, that appears to merge imperceptibly with a sea horizon. This panorama is visible between the south-west and the north-east, beyond which the rising land blocks further views. It does appear, therefore, that the deeply pecked line, also south-west–north-east orientated, is a representation of this distant skyline.

The south-west extreme of the arc described above would be the point on the real horizon for the setting midwinter sun. The point at which the arc drops steeply is to the north-west, where the sun sets at midsummer. The gentle-to-steep south–north variation along the arc may reflect the angle of the sun's pitch before setting between the winter and summer solstices during the solar year. The cup-and-ring motif, in this instance, is probably a symbol for the evening sun.

The visible sun never journeys beyond the north-west until it is 'reborn' in the north-east at the midsummer sunrise. This area of actual skyline, as viewed from this stone, is occupied by the sea, in itself a prehistoric symbol for the Realm of the Dead. Mention was made earlier of a single cup beneath the pecked 'horizon'. This may represent the 'reborn' sun rising in the east after night-journeying beneath the earth – or the sea – having 'died' in the west the previous evening.

We now consider the Brow Moor Cairn. Even disregarding Slab 1, and its amazing rock art, the cairn itself, in the layout of its plan, holds many secrets. The egg-shaped retaining ring of slab stones was geometrically based on a major axis that was south-west–north-east aligned (exactly the same as the pecked 'horizon' on the Hugh Kendall Stone). At right angles, a minor axis gives a south-east–north-west orientation at the broadest part of the 'egg'. A standing stone indicates the south-east end and a now-fallen stone is at the north-west, suggesting a midwinter sunrise and midsummer sunset alignment. The south-west–north-east orientation of the major axis might indicate a midwinter sunset and, in the reverse direction, midsummer sunrise. These orientations are not degree perfect; they are

Fig. 21. The Hugh Kendall Stone, looking west.

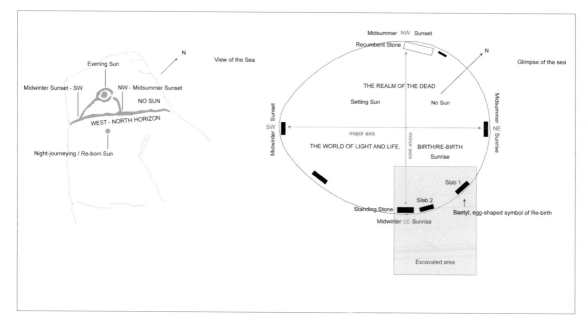

Fig. 22. The Hugh Kendall Stone (left) and Brow Moor Cairn (right). A graphic comparison (not to scale).

probably symbolic, in much the same way that Christian churches and graves are aligned approximately east–west. At the north-north-east, a sliver of sea otherwise blocked by the summit of Stoupe Brow is visible from this cairn. As with the Hugh Kendall Stone, this glimpse lies within the region that the daylight sun never journeys, and is probably significant, revealing, once again, aspects of the Prehistoric Cosmos as if they were deliberately built into the design and location of the monument within the landscape. It must also be mentioned that the 'egg-shaped' plan is quite possibly an intended symbolic reference to birth. In relation to baetyls (egg-shaped stones found at the east of several Irish funerary monuments), one probable decorated example lay to the east of this monument on the old ground surface. Along with a 'reborn' sun in the east, this stone strongly suggests rebirth.

Both the Hugh Kendall Stone and the Brow Moor Cairn appear to be intimately linked with the Prehistoric Cosmos, and with the Realm of the Dead in particular. The aspect from the Hugh Kendall Stone is entirely that of the western horizon, where the sun sets throughout the year. The distant skyline also includes, from the north-west, the entire northern region where the daytime sun never ventures, and this happens to be a sea horizon. West to north, this panorama, and its graphic representation cut in stone, are uncompromising in directing a viewer towards the cosmic Realm of the Dead. Indeed, so selective does the choice of location seem, that views to the east and south are (intentionally?) blocked by a rise in the moor. The Brow Cairn discussed above *is* a funerary monument, and therefore has direct links with the Realm of the Dead, sharing the orientation of the stone. It does not share the same panoramic view, but still manages a glimpse of the North Sea through a dip in the Stoupe Brow summit at the north-north-east. Both the Hugh Kendall Stone and the Brow Cairn appear to symbolise rebirth, an integral part of the 'cosmic equation' (fig. 22).

SUMMARY

If our observations and interpretations are correct, phenomena related both to certain examples of rock motifs in the open landscape, and to stones within circles or other monuments, appear to have a great deal in common, although the timescale for their inception may have stretched over a period of more than 2,000 years – between the Middle Neolithic and the Early Bronze Age. Relating to Northern England, in the examples discussed above, similarities include:

- cardinal orientation and alignments
- calendrical alignments
- deliberate and precise location in relation to the surrounding landscape, and with the position of the sun
- glimpses into a partially shared cosmos

The Early Bronze Age tendency to copy, overlay and add to previous Neolithic rock motifs usually resulted in rock art less sympathetic to the nature of the 'canvas'.

> This Early Bronze Age rock art seems to imitate the phase 1 (*Neolithic*) tradition, but it does not share the same sense of positioning on the rock surface. The design elements are copied, but the existing (*natural*) patterns of the rock are not embellished, implying a lack of understanding of the original carving tradition. (Waddington 2004, 17)

The examples given above, located in an area dubbed the Astro-Geometric Zone, are so different in nature from Neolithic rock art as to imply a totally different purpose and function. Also, these stones appear less weathered and individual peckmarks are still visible, suggesting that they belong to the Early Bronze Age. The Brow Cairn has an apparent counterpart in Ireland – the Millin Bay Cairn near Portaferry, which belongs to the Late Neolithic (Smith and Walker 2008, 39). Evidence from on-the-spot examination of the rock art on Slab 1 and of markings on the baetyl stone of Brow Cairn, however – and also from the study of high definition photographs taken at the excavation – has led the authors to believe that they were made with *metal* tools. This, of course, dates the art to the Early Bronze Age. Perhaps the Hugh Kendall Stone, from which the Brow Cairn is currently visible, was a contemporary. This would explain the apparent similarities.

Finally, we return to the Neolithic Castlerigg Stone Circle, and the precise true-north–south alignment of two portals with a distant mountain crag and a gap in the mountains (see the beginning of chapter). The low midwinter sun would have appeared just above these mountains, and at midday it would have been directly over Dodd Crag. Viewing such an occurrence between the north portals must have been part of the planning of this monument; the sun's appearance here at midday was an indicator, for a few days, that midwinter had been reached (fig. 23).

Interestingly, at night, the constellation of Orion would also have been centred over Dodd Crag at midwinter, as viewed above these portals. The brightest star, Sirius, may

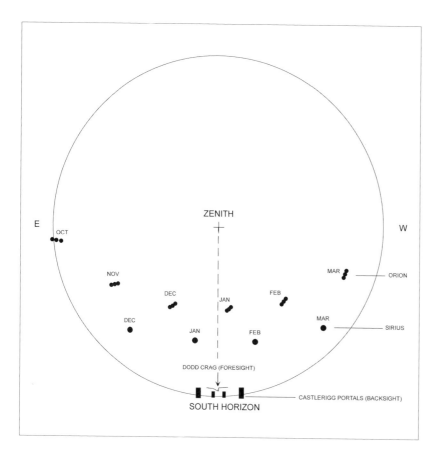

Above: Fig. 23. Castlerigg, showing the 'viewing corridor' between the north and south portals to Dodd Crag in the far distance.

Left: Fig. 24. The winter night sky as viewed between Castlerigg's portals directly south (not to scale). The image shows the apparent east–west progress of Orion's belt and Sirius, the brightest star (compilation based on *Star Finder*, Woodruff & Tirion 2000).

also have been used as a calendrical indicator (fig. 24, col. pl. 9). Indeed, is it possible that Castlerigg began as a long 'four-poster', comprising the two north portals and the two south portals aligned on Dodd Crag and a dip in the mountains, directly to the south? Stones of varying shape and size forming the circle are certainly arranged with approximate symmetry to the east and west of this 'viewing corridor' and could, therefore, have been added later.

If the above suggestions prove to be correct, this does mean contradicting the findings of both Professor Alexander Thom and Aubrey Burl. Neither, in any of their publications, mentions the importance of the southern aspect, and what we believe would amount to the true purpose of this ancient monument. Indeed, and to the contrary, Burl instead stresses the view north beyond the portals (Burl 1979, fig. 8e).

REFERENCES

Burl, A., *The Stone Circles of the British Isles* (London: Yale University Press, 1979).

Burl, A., *A Guide to the Stone Circles of Britain, Ireland and Brittany* (London: Yale University Press, 1995).

Burl, A., *Great Stone Circles*, (Italy: Yale University Press, 1999).

Smith, B. A., and A. A. Walker, *Rock Art and Ritual: Interpreting the Prehistoric Landscapes of the North York Moors* (Stroud: Tempus, 2008).

Waddington, C., 'Rock of Ages' in *British Archaeology* 78 (York: CBA, 2004).

Woodruff, J., and W. Tirion, *Star Finder* (London: George Philip, 2000).

8

Accessing Sunlight – and Deliberate Denial – for Calendrical and Cosmological Purposes

1. EXAMPLES ON THE NORTH YORK MOORS

The Garfit Gap

Notice a row of four cups, with two fainter cups beneath, on the north shoulder of Rock 2 (fig. 25). They only become visible when the sun is high in the sky, approximately between the spring and autumn equinoxes. This period of six months is, of course, summer. Were the six cups used as lunar month counters during this period in order to calculate the return to winter? Organised rows of six or twelve cups (similar to egg trays) have been dubbed 'domino stones' by researcher Stan Beckensall, and are believed by the authors to have been devised for counting lunar months during a solar year. As far as we are aware, no other interpretation has been given for this phenomenon, found not only within the North York Moors, but also at several locations in Northumberland. In locations as far away as southern Sweden, Christopher Tilley has proposed a similar suggestion as to their purpose (Tilley 1999, 146).

If the rows of cups described above were, as we suggest, domino stones, this has implications for the chronology of this type of counter on Fylingdales Moors and Near Moor. As there is no apparent Early Bronze Age presence in Garfit Gap, these cups very probably predate this era and may well be of Neolithic origin. Is this also probable for the Fylingdales Moors and Near Moor domino stones?

Conversely, the west slope of Rock 2 (fig. 26) has soft cups, some with rings, only seen in the low sunlight of the winter months, especially in combination with rainfall and surface water. Weathering may have influenced our interpretation, but we stress such emphasis would have equally applied when the carvings were pristine.

Such configurations of rock motifs relative to the direction of sunlight through the seasons could be the result of pure chance. However, we consider it probable that the locations of rock motifs were deliberately planned from the outset. We have noted that an overwhelming sample of rock motifs within the open landscape are on surfaces where the carvings are enhanced by sunlight, with a particular emphasis on low sunlight creating shadows that enhance the motifs. This occurs throughout the landscapes of northern Britain. Certainly, out of 200 or so carved stones on the Fylingdales Moors above Ravenscar, no north-facing earthfast stones, nor stones on northern slopes, have been selected. Most have aspects towards the south and the west.

Fig. 25. Two rows of cups at Rock 2, Garfit Gap.

Fig. 26. Cup and cup-and-ring motifs on the west slope of Rock 2, Garfit Gap, in December 2001.

The RAF Stone

The cup-and-ring motifs at each end of this east–west orientated earthfast stone on Brow Moor (see chapter seven) are very weathered. This includes the short east-aligned gutter from the central cup of the eastern motif (fig. 27). This shallow motif is only visible in low-angled sunlight during winter, at around midday. Between these cup-and-ring motifs, a pecked north–south line looks sharper and is best seen in low early morning or evening sunlight. As this motif was probably equally exposed to the elements, this suggests that it post-dates the cup and rings. We speculate it was made in the Early Bronze Age, and the pecked north–south linear may therefore demonstrate a continued interest in the cardinal points and a continuance of tradition.

On the same Fylingdales Moors are five more weathered flat stones with short gutters running from (or into) cups at the centre of concentric rings. As with the above example, the gutters are all aligned to cardinal points. Two are directed to the east and three point to the south. All six stones appear to be targeting the sun. The east-aligned gutters are perhaps inviting the rising sun, the cosmic symbol for birth or rebirth, into the centre of their design. The three south-aligned channels may have symbolically 'drawn in energy' when the sun was at its highest and warmest.

Fig. 27. The east-orientated 'gutter' of the Brow Moor RAF Stone.

It is interesting to note that these short 'gutters' do not lead down-slope and cannot, therefore, be associated with water-flow as we believe to be the case where spectacular long grooves on sloping surfaces are found, in Northumberland and Argyll in particular (see chapters four and five). Such 'flow channels' frequently incorporate natural rock fissures. Are we looking at a local phenomenon, peculiar to the Fylingdales Moors?

The Island Comb Stone

As with the RAF Stone, a later motif – a crude cup-and-ring – has been added to this stone on Howdale Moor. It cuts through a series of weathered 'combs', suggesting that the shallow 'combs' belong to an earlier period and had either not been recognised or were deliberately disfigured. Unlike the pecked line on the RAF Stone, this undoubtedly later motif may have been an attempt to emulate the three cups with rings and flow grooves near the base of the boulder. This motif, however, lacked the understanding and sensitivity of the work of the earlier exponent(s). Nearby are marked 'portables', which may have been dispersed from Early Bronze Age barrows or cairns, suggesting a temporal association. The earlier fine, parallel 'combs', 'hanging' from natural horizontal fissures, require a precise angle of sunlight in late afternoon around midsummer for them to become visible, preferably in combination with surface water. The choice of the azimuth and angle of surface was probably intentional (fig. 28).

Fig. 28. A crude cup-and-ring cuts through earlier 'combs'.

Three Stones Associated with a Small Cairn

In 2007, the authors assisted Blaise Vyner in the excavation of a small cairn on Brow Moor (Vyner 2007, 25). Although structured to some extent, there was no definite evidence of funerary activity. Close enough to appear associated with the cairn were three stones that had, at some time, been brought to the site. Their upper surfaces had cups that, although weathered, still showed peckmarks in several instances. These stones were turned to reveal rock carvings that had the appearance of water-flow features on their undersides. These were not weathered and had, therefore, probably been created, or selected, for the purpose of facing downward into the ground. Were these stones a cosmological link between the underworld, the Realm of the Dead where sunlight was deliberately denied, and the world of light and life above?

II. BEYOND THE NORTH YORK MOORS

Spirals in Northumberland and Lothian

Earlier, we suggested that spiral motifs probably symbolised entry into the Realm of the Dead (see Dronfield 1997). They are usually found on the vertical rock surfaces of megalithic monuments, especially passage tombs such as Newgrange and Knowth. These rare open-landscape examples are carved on vertical natural cliff faces beside rivers. Both sets of motifs are north-facing and are therefore denied direct sunlight (see above), but do not appear to be associated with funerary monuments. Both rivers, the North Esk and the Coquet, are in their 'old age' stages before they 'die' as they flow into the tidal salt water of the sea. Was veneration for the 'life' of a river sufficiently important to carve these motifs in such difficult, even dangerous, places? Were the cremated remains of the dead placed into sacred rivers, as is still the practice in India and Nepal (col. pl. 10, fig. 29)? There is evidence for such practice during our Neolithic and Early Bronze Age (Bradley 2007, 202).

Newgrange

Also by the lower reaches of a river, in this case the Boyne in eastern Ireland, are several passage tombs. The reconstructed Newgrange (if a true reconstruction of the original monument) is massive, magnificent and older than the pyramids of Ancient Egypt. It has also concealed an internal secret for 5,000 years.

Entry into the dark and mysterious interior of Newgrange may have been for the selected few. Accounts of recent visitors describe experiences of total isolation, even sensory deprivation, in progressing along the south-east–north-west-aligned passage leading into the end chambers. It seems probable that this monument had been constructed to symbolise the journey into the underworld, the Realm of the Dead (Dronfield 1997, Devereux 2006) from which the sun was denied entry (see above). In 1963, the excavation team led by Michael O'Kelly discovered a 'light-box' above the

Fig. 29. Linked spirals on a cliff above the River Coquet, Morwick, Northumberland.

formerly sealed entrance to the monument. When investigated, this stone arrangement profoundly demonstrated that controlled denial of, and access to, sunlight was designed into this monument from the outset. Available natural light was controlled in order to create spectacular effects for cosmological purposes. **Only at sunrise on the midwinter solstice** were the sun's rays allowed to enter Newgrange via the 'light-box' and along the south-east–north-west passage in order to light up the inner chamber. It has been calculated that 5,000 years ago (at the time of construction), the beam of sunlight would have bisected the chamber and illuminated a triple spiral carved on the rear orthostat of the end recess (Waddell 2000, 61). Again we encounter linked spirals, but in this instance on the vertical surface of a monument associated with death and the underworld (see also Thomas 1999, 50).

Variations on a Theme

A similar alignment has been confirmed for Maes How in the Orkney Islands. Here it is the **setting** rays of the sun at the midwinter solstice that light up the end chamber (Ashmore 2000, 74).

As recently as 2005, Steve Burrow, curator of Neolithic archaeology at Amgueddfa Cymru (the National Museum of Wales), entered the inner chamber of Bryn Celli Ddu, a passage tomb on Anglesey. He was guided by an observation made by Sir Norman Lockyer, a distinguished scientist who, in 1906, published the first systematic study of megalithic astronomy (Lockyer 1906, 427). At the time, Lockyer's belief that Bryn Celli Ddu's interior passage was aligned with **the summer solstice sunrise** was met with a great deal of scepticism. Burrow, having failed the previous year because of cloud cover, was able to confirm on midsummer's morning, 2005, that the sun's rays do indeed light up a quartz-rich stone at the back of the tomb (Pitts 2006, 6). Lynch (1991, 98) has noted the apparent relevance of quartz as a construction material within important parts of passage graves, and in particular within Bryn Celli Ddu.

Although the timing varies, these geographically widely-dispersed passage tombs were each denied the entry of the sun's rays for *at least* 360 days every year. 'Special effects' must have been designed into the structure of such monuments from the outset. Whether sunrise or sunset, the summer solstice or the winter solstice, these are major events of calendrical and cosmological importance that mark the crucial turning points of the year in the world of light, the living and fertility. These events may have been seen as the times of year for remembering the ancestors. Perhaps they were an annual celebration of the continuity of existence. The 'theatre' of experience within these passage tombs, as if arranged (for a select few?) by divine forces, must have been overwhelming, especially for people who revered the sun and sunlight as a crucial part of their cosmological belief system, and saw it as essential to life itself.

All of the above passage tombs have spiral motifs on vertical rock surfaces, either within or at their periphery. In 1995, a photograph taken by Hanna Casement unexpectedly revealed a large, clockwise spiral on the inside vertical surface of one of Castlerigg Stone Circle's hard, local metamorphic slate boulders. So fine is this

Cumbrian motif that it can only be seen in exceptional lighting conditions (the motif is west-facing and within a 'box' of boulders inside the circle). Both Stan Beckensall and Paul Brown have succeeded in making rubbings of the spiral, but neither have actually seen it (Beckensall 2002, 74).

SUMMARY

All of the above observations, be they in the open landscape or within megalithic monuments, build a strong case for deliberate planning and organisation during the Neolithic, resulting in a remarkable degree of accuracy for alignments in relation to the angle of the sun's rays. This also included 'designing in' light denial for periods of time. In certain instances, light and the gaze of the living were permanently denied. If these were the result of pure chance, we would not expect to find examples of 'light manipulation' repeated, particularly in the passage tomb instances. To find even one example of designed-in light access would be remarkable; to find this phenomenon repeated in three geographically diverse locations is tantamount to proof of Neolithic intentions.

ADDENDUM

Calendrical or cosmological? Such distinctions would have almost certainly been irrelevant within a culture that embraced both the outer world of survival and the inner world of spirituality and cosmological understanding. There may have been no mental separation between one and the other, as is the case within existing so-called 'primitive' cultures.

Using the same 'tools' of symbolism, metaphor and allegory, the native people of Australia (Clark 2003) and North America (Young 1990 and Milner 2004), for example, led rich lives, guided by their seeing life at both of these levels (pragmatic and spiritual) as being totally intertwined. This is true even in recent history. Indeed, using the descriptions given by direct-line descendants of these people, anthropologists have found that many still adhere to the ancient cosmologies set down in folklore.

REFERENCES

Ashmore, P. J., *Neolithic and Bronze Age Scotland* (London: Babford, 2000).
Beckensall, S., *Prehistoric Rock Art in Cumbria: Landscapes and Monuments* (Stroud: Tempus, 2002).
Bradley, R., *Prehistory of Britain and Ireland* (Cambridge University Press, 2002).
Bradley, R., *Image and Audience: Rethinking Prehistoric Art* (Oxford University Press, 2009).
Clark, P., *Where the Ancestors Walked* (Crows Nest: Allen & Unwin, 2003).
Devereux, P., 'Ears and Years: Aspects of Acoustics and Intentionality' in *Archaeoacoustics*, ed. C. Scarre and G. Lawson, pp. 23–30 (Cambridge: McDonald Institute for Archaeological Research, 2006).
Dronfield, J., 'Entering Alternative Realities: Cognition, Art and Architecture in Irish Passage Tombs', in *Cambridge Archaeological Journal* 1, pp. 37–72 (1997).

Lockyer, N., *Stonehenge and Other British Stone Monuments Astronomically Considered* (London: Macmillan & Co., 1906).

Lynch, F., *Prehistoric Anglesey* (Llangefni: Anglesey Antiquarium Society, 1991).

Milner, G. R., *The Moundbuilders* (London: Thames & Hudson, 2004).

Pitts, M., 'Sensational New Discoveries at Bryn Celli Ddu' in *British Archaeology* 89, p. 6 (2006).

Smith, B. A., 'Recent Discoveries of Prehistoric Rock Motifs: The Wainstones Site' in *Yorkshire Archaeological Journal* 75, p. 3 (2003).

Thomas, J., *Understanding the Neolithic* (London: Routledge, 1999).

Tilley, C., *Metaphor and Material Culture* (Oxford: Blackwell, 1999).

Vyner, B., 'Fylingdales Moor, North Yorkshire, 2007' in *Forum: CBA Yorkshire Annual Newsletter 2008* pp. 25–7 (2007).

Waddell, J., *The Prehistoric Archaeology of Ireland* (Wicklow: Wordwell Ltd, 2003).

Waddington, C., 'Neolithic Rock Art in the British Isles: Retrospect and Prospect' in *Art as Metaphor*, ed. A. Mazel, G. Nash, and C. Waddington, pp. 49–68 (Oxford: Archaeopress, 2007).

Young, M. J., *Signs from the Ancestors* (Albuquerque: University of New Mexico Press, 1990).

Conclusion to Part Two

In parallel with rainfall, water and water-flow (see part one), Neolithic rock art (some belonging to the Early Bronze Age) offers convincing evidence that sunlight played a major part in the creation of certain kinds of motifs.

The location of such motifs on the surface of a rock, or within the surrounding landscape, in relation to the position of the sun appears to have been just as important as the motifs themselves. Neolithic monuments such as passage tombs or stone circles also had designed-in alignments with the sun, in relation to key calendrical/cosmological events. Some passage tombs were designed to allow access to sunlight for only a day or so each year (see chapter eight). In many instances, usually in funerary contexts, sunlight in relation to rock art was permanently denied, the motifs facing inwards or downwards as if in communication with the Realm of the Dead. Such understanding of the direction of the sun's rays in relation to open-landscape rock art and megalithic monuments may well have been used as a form of power and control over the minds of the general populace. Did religious leaders manipulate these 'special effects'?

Major construction programmes took place during the Neolithic within diverse regions of the British Isles. Hugely impressive stone circles were created: the Ring of Brodgar, the Standing Stones of Stenness and the Callanish Stones in the Northern Isles; the Cumbrian circles of Castlerigg, Long Meg and Swinside; the southern circles of Avebury and Stonehenge in Wiltshire. By the River Boyne in eastern Ireland, the massive passage tombs of Knowth and Newgrange were constructed even before the pyramids in Ancient Egypt. Maes Howe in the far north on Orkney and Bryn Celli Ddu on Anglesey are two further widely-dispersed examples of passage tombs.

Within these monuments are designed-in alignments that relate directly to the position of the sun at pivotal times of year. Such immense undertakings were not embarked upon without careful forethought, both as to their structure and with regard to their orientation and location within the landscape. Standing for 5,000 years, these monuments remain as indisputable evidence that the sun was an integral part of a relationship with the cyclical passage of time. In parallel with – or even in conjunction with – water and water-flow, the cycles of the sun, whether daily or annually, also became a metaphor linked with the constant renewal of life that existed within the Neolithic mind. Lesser monuments and certain forms of rock art within the British Isles are telling us the same stories – some continuing into the Early Bronze Age.

PART THREE

MINDSCAPES

Introduction to Part Three

The world that we see around us is a figment of the imagination, the result of a lifetime of learning and of conditioning within whatever culture, or sub-culture, we happen to have been born into. Language, be it an evocation of sound, taste, texture, smell or vision, is the means by which the 'outer' world is ultimately interpreted, and as a consequence it becomes 'reality'. 'What is its name?' 'Draw a picture of it.' These are two powerful aspects of language by which a child increasingly comes to terms with the external world. Throughout life, ever more sophisticated language enables us to 'get a handle' not only on that which can be seen or touched, but also on abstract concepts. In order to enter this realm, and to fix ideas in the mind, the use of symbols, metaphors and allegories come into play. This is the way that the mind works. 5,000 years ago this would have been exactly the same.

In the 'civilised' twenty-first-century western world, our minds have been conditioned to separate the 'real' from the imaginary, the tangible from the abstract. We see things as if in separate compartments: science, medicine, religion, art, politics, earning a living etc. This has not always been so. As described in Native American Elder Annie York's *They Write Their Dreams on the Rock Forever* (York, Daly and Arnett 1993), a lifestyle can be imagined that blends or merges all aspects of life. The Native American people communicated in a variety of ways: words and stories, rock art, signs by pathways, hand signs, smoke signals, music and dance etc. 'Fact' and 'fiction' were probably not concepts that they would have readily understood. They lived in a world of myth and magic, handed down from ancestors, that explained every aspect of life, including birth and death. Their relationship with the world around them, especially with other living creatures, the elements and the seasons, were part-and-parcel of the folklore handed down through the generations.

All that writing there in the Stein! I don't blame the Indians wants to preserve it. It tells you from the beginning of this earth, when the earth was young, and these persons smart enough to write it in there, what they dream. That was the way it began.

The fainter, diagonal line right across the drawing, with linked circles on it?

Well, sure! That's the passing of time. One, two, three, four. Five, six, seven. Eight, nine, ten, eleven. Eleven suns have risen. Each one is a sun making its full journey over the day. (York, Daly and Arnett, 107)

Annie is explaining the meaning of a group of rock 'writings' (pictograms) in the Stein River Valley of British Columbia. If only we had an Annie York to decipher the rock art of Northern England! Would she have given similar meaning to the Hugh Kendall Stone on Brow Moor (chapter seven) or to the six- and twelve-cup domino stones, of which there are several on the North York Moors? The latter are believed by the authors to be devices for counting lunar months throughout a solar year.

It does seem that prehistoric rock art in Britain and Ireland can be divided into two categories, with very little overlap. The rock art of the open landscape, as might be expected, appears to be concerned with aspects of life: rainfall, sunlight, birth and rebirth, the flow of water and the flow of time. A second category, mainly associated with funerary monuments, is very different in nature. Here, a range of symbols is linked with the Realm of the Dead. The motifs from either category are fairly consistent throughout the geographical areas mentioned above, with some regional variation. This is a different division to the ideas expressed in parts one and two. The 'surgeon's knife' can cut in several ways. As mentioned in parts one and two, a further partitioning might take the rock art of the Neolithic and Early Bronze Age and define, then separate, the characteristics of motifs associated with each time period.

All such analytical ways of seeing the past are to an extent valid. But they may be construed as being little more than an academic exercise and an obsession with partitioning, categorising – offering neat, tight definitions. Indeed, it is the use of such 'boxes' for storing information that is one of the major failings of twenty-first-century civilisation. The tighter we fit ideas, things and people into stereotyping 'boxes', the further we become removed from any real hope of truly understanding not only the workings of the prehistoric mind, but also solutions to our own current problems. Solutions often lie within the transition zones between categories.

We here cite David Lewis-Williams and David Pearce in *Inside the Neolithic Mind*:

Archaeologists have expended much energy in classifying megalithic tombs according to shape, size and so forth. Sometimes the passage or the end chamber may have smaller side chambers, thus giving it a cruciform shape. End chambers without side alcoves are known as undifferentiated tombs. Those with demarcated spaces are called 'court tombs'. Classificatory work of this kind illustrates a curious principle in archaeological research. When we cannot explain, we classify – in ever increasing detail. Though understandable given the daunting nature of research, the whole task of classification can become self-defeating. Classification demands the selection of criteria. Necessarily, the selection of criteria is done 'blind': in doing so, researchers may emphasize features that had little or nothing to do with the significance that the items being classified had for their makers and users. Unless researchers luckily hit on criteria that were significant, each classification moves them further and further away from the original meaning of the items. But once researchers have some grasp of that meaning, they can construct a much more instructive (and probably simpler) classification. (Lewis-Williams and Pearce 2005, 181)

REFERENCES

Lewis-Williams, D., and D. Pearce, *Inside the Neolithic Mind* (London: Thames & Hudson, 2005).

Longfellow, H. W., *The Song of Hiawatha* in *The Story of Hiawatha: Re-told from Longfellow*, ed. C. E. Whitaker, p. 59 (Leeds: E. J. Arnold & Son, 1855)

York, A., R. Daly, and C. Arnett, *They Write Their Dreams on the Rock Forever* (Vancouver: Talonbooks, 1993).

9

Deciphering Rock Art in Northern England (With Reference to Examples Further Afield)

Based on the authors' personal observations and interpretations, we now attempt to 'do an Annie York' by selecting specific rock motifs that are generally well represented throughout the British Isles, but with a strong bias towards the North of England – our main area of research. Our 'surgeon's knife' separates the purpose, meaning and characteristics of rock art found within the open landscape from that associated with funerary monuments. As explained above, overlap does occur, although it is limited to a few examples, and the division between the Neolithic and the Early Bronze Age is not always clear-cut. We hope to paint a broad but intimate picture, as may have been envisaged by people living 4,000–5,000 years ago through one of their still-surviving forms of language and of communication. It must be stressed that rock motifs often have more than one purpose or meaning, which is dependent on such factors as their contextual location in landscape, within a monument or in relation to the elements, the cosmological beliefs of the artist, and the passage of time.

ROCK MOTIFS WITHIN THE OPEN LANDSCAPE

• **Simple cups**, with apparently random distribution, usually on flat or gently sloping rock surfaces, are the most common of motifs within the open landscape. They appear to be indicators of direction, suggesting, for example, an association with ancient pathways or corridors of movement (which are no longer in existence in most cases). This is particularly the case within elevated locations within the North York Moors. This is because of their linear distribution patterns and the choice of terrain, avoiding steep climbs and boggy areas in particular (Walker and Smith, 46–7). Such stones would, no doubt, have given a hunter or herder a sense of reassurance, a feeling of confidence in travelling such routes, knowing that they were travelling in the footsteps of the ancestors. The way had long been tried and tested.

Cups are also frequently associated with 'water features', be they natural, modified or artificially cut into stone. They are often found around 'basins', or beside (or within) 'flow channels', as if in recognition, even in veneration, of a water source and water-flow.

• **Domino cups**, organised rows of cups, especially in groups of six or twelve, are to be found at several locations within the North York Moors, usually on horizontal or gently sloping surfaces (fig. 30). We believe that these domino stones are prehistoric counting devices for recording the number of lunar months within a solar year, even though they fall short of synchronisation by eleven days. Such stones are to be found in Northumberland (at Lordenshaw, for example) and much further afield, in Sweden. Regarding the latter location, Chris Tilley writes:

> I shall argue that they (the rock carvings) are intimately connected, like the representational designs, with movement – but in this case the movement of celestial bodies – and in particular the passage of the seasons. On a number of carving surfaces the cup marks are clearly arranged in sequences and multiples of six and twelve. It is not hard to suggest that this may be related to lunar cycles or years, given the common preoccupation with the passage of the seasons and solar and lunar observation in small scale agricultural societies. (Tilley 1999, 146)

• Also probably associated with the moon are two stones on Howdale Moor in Fylingdales parish, North York Moors. These are only about 20 metres apart, and are apparently linked by small cupstones at regular intervals. Both stones have seven parallel straight grooves and an offset eighth. One has very weathered grooves on the flat top of the stone, the other has sharp, incised lines on a steeply sloping surface. Both stones have three or four cups in close proximity to the grooves. They could easily have functioned as **'Moon-phase calculators'**, thereby establishing a sequence of four lunar weeks within a synodic month (fig. 30).

Whether through the devices of domino stones or Moon-phase calculators, monthly or daily recordings must have involved such processes as re-scouring, pigment application and/or the placement of objects (quartz pebbles?) within the rock indentations. Was someone of shamanic status entrusted with the task of keeping a record of the daily, weekly, monthly and yearly recurrence of solar and lunar events? The local populace may well have approached such a 'time-keeper' in order to plan ahead for planting and harvesting, breeding and culling, hunting and gathering. The seasons and the Prehistoric Cosmos were time-dependent and inextricably interlinked. Should sea travel have been envisaged, there was probably a 'safe' time of year for doing so. The tides were linked with the phases of the moon, as with the female menstrual cycle. Social events may well have taken place at designated times in the year. The use of such stones for recording, calculating and predicting was certainly far more than an academic exercise.

• **Cup-and-ring motifs** are far from straightforward. They appear to carry within their symbolism a variety of meanings, including more than one meaning in a single motif. Their location within the landscape, perhaps tied with the sun's position, or with rainfall and water-flow and with the Prehistoric Cosmos, are crucial factors in determining purpose or meaning. The authors are convinced that these stones are representational, either at the directly visual level, or as symbols representing abstract ideas.

The 'pure drop' – the transfer of water from the sky (the prehistoric upper cosmos layer or sphere) onto an elevated ground surface – was probably seen as water at its very purest, as suggested in chapter four. In existing water, within pools or 'basins', raindrops create

Fig. 30. *Top:* Twelve-cup domino stone, Near Moor. *Below:* A Moon-phase calculator, Howdale Moor.

Fig. 31. Chatton Park, showing the proximity of a cup-and-ring motif to a natural basin.

concentric rings of water ripples (fig. 9). In hill country, especially above the spring line, such an occurrence may well have been seen as the 'birth' of a rivulet or stream. Taking this notion a step further, the raindrop with concentric rings may have become a symbol for birth itself. Are we taking the argument too far in further suggesting that the initial (pure) raindrop became a symbol for the 'soul', born but a fraction before the 'body' and seen as a surrounding ring or rings? (Later, we will discover that carved rings *without cups* are strongly associated with funerary monuments and the Realm of the Dead.)

Is, therefore, the carved cup with surrounding ring(s) – which is so frequently found within elevated locations within the hill country of Northern England (and beyond) – a symbol for birth, incorporating the abstract concept of body and soul? Additionally, grooves and channels linking the inner cup with 'the world beyond the outer ring' are a frequent occurrence and appear to add weight to our hypothesis. There may also be a direct link here with stone circles (see chapter six).

• **Flow channels** are frequently associated with both 'basins' and cup-and-ring motifs in hill locations (fig. 31). Basins are natural, modified or artificially cut. There are many examples of all types at elevated locations within the North York Moors and in Northumberland. Characteristically, most basins show both 'inflow' and 'outflow' channels – suggesting the importance of the transfer of water from rainfall above and the continuing flow towards the valleys below. Most locations have, today, dramatic or extensive views into valleys, plains or even the sea (col. pl. 2, 11).

Basins are referred to above as containers of water into which a 'pure drop' of rain might fall and momentarily create a series of concentric rings. Observation of this phenomenon may have led to the carving of rocks in order to create replicas, as if the phenomenon were 'frozen in time'. These are the motifs we now know as cup-and-ring. Interestingly, natural or modified basins are frequently found in close proximity to cup-and-ring motifs (fig. 31).

Many cup-and-ring motifs have channels deliberately cut to lead down-slope from their inner cups (fig. 31). There can be little doubt that such channels were created to allow water to flow from its source.

Rock art, particularly in Northumberland, has taken this notion of water-flow into the realms of pure sculpture, as if transforming rocks into 'fossilised' or 'frozen' streams or rivers in full flow (see chapter five and col. pl. 4, 5, 12).

From their 'birth' in the hills, rivulets, streams and rivers must surely have become symbols for 'the flow of life'. Such symbolism was clearly intended and explains one aspect of cup-and-ring motifs – that of their association with water and water-flow.

- **Short grooves** or '**gutters**' – again linking the inner cup with the world outside the outer ring of cup-and-ring motifs – must have served a different symbolic purpose to the long down-slope flow channels discussed above.

There are at least six cup-and-ring motifs with short 'gutters' on elevated moorland above Robin Hood's Bay, at the extreme eastern edge of the North York Moors. The east–west-orientated earthfast RAF Stone on Brow Moor (see chapter seven) has such a groove, extremely weathered. It is directed towards the east from the cup at the centre of the eastern cup-and-ring motif. Two other approximately east-aligned 'gutters' occur on Brow Moor. Also on Brow Moor are two further cup-and-ring motifs with short grooves aligned to the south, as is another on Howdale Moor. All these motifs are very weathered, requiring low-angled sunlight to cast sufficient shadow for them to become clearly visible. The probability is, because of extreme weathering, that these motifs belong to some point within the Neolithic period.

These 'gutters' do not usually lead downhill, as is the case with flow channels. It is within their orientations that we suspect a clue as to their purpose or meaning. As is frequently mentioned throughout this volume, the rising sun in the east was probably a symbol of birth or rebirth. Also, the sun rises to its highest point in the sky, directly south, at midday. It does seem probable that cup-and-ring motifs with 'gutters' were deliberately aligned toward the sun, as if to draw the power from its rays into the very centre of these carved motifs, in order, perhaps, to energise the 'soul' – the symbolic centre cup.

- The cup-and-ring motif may, in certain cases, represent the sun itself. In chapter seven, we considered the Early Bronze Age Hugh Kendall Stone on Brow Moor, and argued that its cup-and-ring motif represented the evening sun, with the arc indicating the angle of the sun's pitch to the horizon during its setting at different points in the year. The south-western limit, then, indicates the midwinter sunset; the most north-westerly point the midsummer sunset (see page 58).

Fig. 32. Grid stone, Brow Moor.

There are still many aspects of cup-and-ring stones that remain a mystery. Why, for instance, are some cups encircled by a single ring, or even a gapped ring (or penannular), while others, particularly in Northumberland and at Kilmartin in Argyll, boast many concentric rings? Might this be simply a matter of regional variation and artistic exuberance, or is further meaning encoded within the number of these rings?

• **Grid motifs** vary greatly in their designs. These rare stones incorporate cups or cup-and-ring motifs and are carved into sloping or near-vertical surfaces. We know of only five examples within the North York Moors: two on Brow Moor, one at Allan Tofts near Goathland, and two at the north-west fringes in Garfit Gap (fig. 32, col. pl. 13).

There are other stones with carved squares or rectangles, but these do not interlock in the same manner to form a grid pattern.

It is the location of the above stones within the landscape that appears to be a common denominator. They are all the first stones to be encountered after climbing a slope above boggy areas. They are positioned at or near the 'shoulder', where elevated ground begins to level out, and they are tilted, or are on a vertical surface, as if to face the hill walker. In other words, it appears that these stones *wanted* to be encountered. This sample size is too small, however, to be reliable.

In all cases, the elevated ground above the grid stones appear to have been 'special places', if the large amount of rock art to be found there is anything to go by. Could these stones have been symbolic gateways (or barriers) to the 'rock art galleries' that lay beyond?

ROCK MOTIFS AND FUNERARY MONUMENTS

It is not only the nature of rock art associated with the Realm of the Dead that is fundamentally different to examples described above in the open landscape, **but also its position on the rock surface.** Most motifs in this second category are found on vertical surfaces, whereas the vast majority within the open landscape are on horizontal or sloping surfaces. Also, rock art in the open was invariably positioned so that the rays of the sun, at various times of day, or during the year, were able to pick out the carved motifs. Funerary rock art, by contrast, was often denied light for much of the year, or was sealed or inverted so that the sun's rays, and the gaze of the living, were permanently denied access (see chapter eight).

• **The spiral** may be the *antithesis* of the open landscape cup-and-ring motif (chapter four). We have argued that the cup-and-ring motif symbolised not only the birth of a stream, but also the actual birth of the body and soul (see above). By contrast, the spiral may have its origins in the dangerous vortices of whirlpools – of which Neolithic seafarers navigating the Scottish west coast would have been only too aware (see chapter four). Also related to the sea are fossilised seashells. Spiralling ammonites must have presented a real puzzle to prehistoric people, no doubt suggesting possible links with 'another world'. Interestingly, a huge ammonite embedded in a slab of stone must surely have been deliberately chosen as an entrance portal at Stoney Littleton Chambered Cairn, near the River Avon in Somerset. Both of these possible sources for spiral motifs are directly linked with the sea, and therefore the Earth's underworld and Realm of the Dead, seen as the lower layer (or sphere) of the Prehistoric Cosmos.

The spiral may also have been a representation of things experienced in altered states of consciousness, particularly with regard to 'near-death experiences'. Frequently, recollections refer to a 'tunnel' or 'spiralling vortex' with a welcoming light at the end. Within the mind, the spiral may have given symbolic visual form to the inner 'soul' turning away from the world of light and life, and, irreversibly, turning inwards as death approached. The spiral, therefore, was probably a powerful, even frightening, symbol for entry into the Realm of the Dead.

In chapter eight, we saw that several passage tombs built in the Neolithic period are known to have carved spiral motifs. Newgrange and Knowth, on the Bend in the Boyne in eastern Ireland, are perhaps the best-known examples. Spirals also occur within two passage tombs on Anglesey, and, much further afield, at Maes How in the Orkney Islands. These are all undisputedly funerary monuments. Two stone circles of the same period on the western side of Northern England, in Cumbria, are also known to have spirals. At Long Meg, the motifs are very weathered and located on the vertical surface of this huge stone circle 'outlier'. In chapter four, Burl was cited as recognising a midwinter sunset association (which was symbolically linked with entry into the Realm of the Dead):

> Long Meg, therefore, may possess one of the first megalithic symbols to be understood in modern times. (Burl 1999, 40)

Recently, within the Castlerigg Circle, a large spiral was discovered by photography in ideal conditions and later confirmed by rubbings. Again, it is on a vertical, in this case a west-facing stone surface (i.e. towards the sunset). Few have actually *seen* this spiral, so slight is the depth of its engraving (see chapter eight).

So far, so good – the spiral is consistently linked with either funerary monuments, or within stone circle monuments where the choice of location strongly suggests a link with the dying setting sun in the west. Strangely, spirals have also been discovered in open-landscape contexts with no apparent association with funerary or other monuments. Even here, there are parallels with the monuments mentioned above. At Morwick, by the River Coquet in Northumberland, and by the River North Esk in Lothian, south-east Scotland – both near the east coast of Britain – there are spirals (and other motifs) on vertical cliffs:

- In order to access these sites, difficult, even dangerous, scrambles (including outright rock-climbing in some cases) are necessary. These sites are cut off from the surrounding world. Most passage tombs can only be accessed with difficulty and from the inside – total isolation.
- Both of these 'natural' sites face towards the north, and are therefore denied the sun's rays for most of the year. It is only at high summer, around sunrise or sunset, that the sun illuminates some of these motifs (see chapter eight).
- Both sites are beside the lower reaches of rivers (in their 'old age' stage, shortly before their 'dying' in the tidal salt waters of the sea), as at the Bend in the Boyne.

As we asked earlier, was the imminent 'death of a river' of sufficient cosmological importance for Neolithic people to risk life and limb in carving these motifs on sheer cliff-faces at considerable height, in many cases above a river? The topography of these riverside landscapes may have changed in 5,000 years, but 5,000 years from the end of the last Ice Age, sea level in relation to land-rise was stabilising, suggesting a similar physical appearance as seen today. The rock artists were therefore taking considerable risks that only experienced rock-climbers with state-of-the-art equipment would attempt today (fig. 33).

As we suggested in chapter eight, there may have been a tradition during the Neolithic that has parallels today in India and Nepal, where the cremated remains of bodies are disposed of in rivers. There is no proof of such activity by the banks of the Coquet or North Esk, but it would explain a lack of funerary sites for the 'general populace' during the Neolithic, and account for rock art associated with death at these two open-landscape locations.

- Geometric shapes such as **lozenges, triangles, chevrons and zigzags**, as with the spiral, are found in association with funerary monuments both in Ireland and Britain. Such motifs appear to deliberately contradict the gentler curvilinear rock art found within open-landscape contexts, even within the same geographical regions. Using both acute and obtuse angles, such severe geometric forms might suggest something rather

Left: Fig. 33. Climbers at Morwick.

Below: Fig. 34. Lozenges, triangles, chevrons and zigzags on Slab 1, Brow Moor Cairn.

Fig. 35. Lozenge motif on Castlerigg Circle boulder.

terrible, even frightening – as indeed an association with death may well have been perceived during the Neolithic and the Early Bronze Age (fig. 34).

The lozenge may have its origins in the negative space between four spirals, as on the magnificent stone at the entrance to Newgrange (fig. 11). Likewise, the other angular shapes could have developed from such a source. None relate to the world of light and life; they instead suggest links with the underworld and with death.

Again we find vertical rock surfaces being favoured for such artwork, but rarely outside the context of funerary monuments. At Castlerigg in 1995, however, two students from Newcastle University, Nick Best and Neil Stevenson, photographed the elusive spiral on the inner, western face of a circle stone. Later, they discovered a lozenge motif incised into a boulder at the west of the circle (fig. 35).

• **Concentric rings without a central cup** are commonly found within passage tombs. Single rings without a central cup occasionally occur in the open landscape. Returning to the cliffs at Morwick beside the Coquet (see above), and the rare location of spirals in the open landscape, we also find another apparent association with the Realm of the Dead. High up, on vertical cliff faces, are several double rings without cups (fig. 36).

Earlier in this chapter, we suggested that the cup-and-ring motif in open hill country may have been a symbol for the birth of body and soul, the cup representing the soul and the surrounding ring the body. If our theory is correct, then it follows that rings without a central cup are the antithesis – a symbol for the body *without* a soul – i.e. a dead body.

It is important to mention the recent inland discovery near Chapel Stile, Cumbria, of a rock art frieze on the vertical eastern face of a huge block of Andesite tuff. A series of concentric rings, without cups, occupies the lower parts of the surface. Chevrons are also present. 'Rising' above are several deep cups. If our analogy is correct, these may represent souls released from the bodies below. Great Langdale Beck is currently less than 100 metres away to the west (Beckensall 2002, 34–47).

Fig. 36. Concentric rings without cups, Morwick.

We have argued that all of the above symbols, found within funerary monuments, or occasionally at other sites (see above), are directly linked to death and entry into the Realm of the Dead. Light denial, isolation, 'dying' sunsets and 'dying' river symbolism, appear to have played a powerful part in the 'special effects department' of this prehistoric 'theatre of death'.

• So far we have been dealing with motifs on rocks that were either earthfast within the open landscape or on stones forming the structure of monuments. In relation to the latter are **portables**, small stones that have been brought to funerary sites and deposited beside or within them. Such portables may have been offerings to the deceased and frequently had only one or two cups carved into them, although many were more elaborately carved. It seems, because of their weathered appearance, that some of these stones had been broken from rock art panels within the open landscape. The practice of bringing portable stones to funerary sites was widespread throughout the Britain and in Ireland during the Neolithic, and continued into the Early Bronze Age.

One particular type of portable is the egg-shaped baetyl stone, some examples of which have markings, while others do not. What is of interest in relation to these rounded stones is that they have been found on or in the old ground surface, outside the main body of funerary monuments and invariably on the eastern side. In chapter four of our first volume, we argued that the egg was a symbol for birth and that in combination

with the sun rising in the east, baetyls may well have been ritually placed in order to
ensure the rebirth of the souls of the deceased (fig. 43).

SUMMARY

The map below (fig. 37), centred on Northern England – where the majority of our rock
art research has taken place – shows the location of most sites mentioned in the text.

What is immediately apparent is the distribution of funerary sites with rock art. Apart
from the Brow Moor Cairn on the east coast of Northern England, these monuments,
with their distinct style of rock art, are confined to the fringes of the Irish Sea and Loch
Fynne, north of the Kilbrannan Sound.

Both the Castlerigg and Long Meg Neolithic stone circles have motifs that are
usually associated with funerary monuments; both are located in the west of Northern
England, in Cumbria. The influence of the Irish Sea culture could easily have penetrated

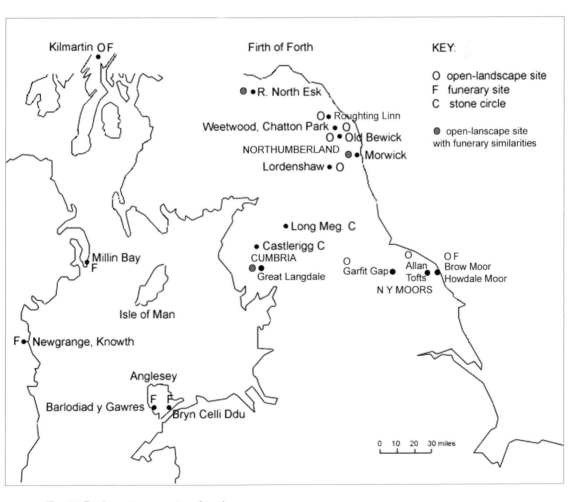

Fig. 37. Rock art sites mentioned in the text.

such distances inland. In the first volume of *Rock Art and Ritual*, we made a case for at least one west–east overland route linking the North York Moors and the Brow Moor Cairn with the Irish Sea (Smith and Walker 2008, 41–3). It is more difficult to explain the two open-landscape sites, one beside the River North Esk, Lothian, and the other at Morwick, Northumberland, beside the River Coquet. Both sites have rock art similar to that associated with funerary monuments in close proximity to the Irish Sea, however, in common with the Brow Moor Cairn, they could not be further away, at the eastern extremes of the British mainland. Somehow, by land or by sea, links must have been forged.

The recent discovery of an open-landscape rock with iconic imagery apparently related to Irish passage tombs at Chapel Stile in Great Langdale, Cumbria, gives further food for thought.

In 1993, Scandinavian archaeologist Bo Graslund delivered his prestigious Europa Lecture to the Prehistoric Society, entitled 'Prehistoric Soul Beliefs in Northern Europe'. His research paper leaves little doubt that prehistoric settled communities recognised the funerary separation of soul from body under a variety of ritual conditions from the Early Neolithic (Graslund 1994, 15–26). Rock art symbolism is not mentioned, nor the possible placement of cremated bodies into water. Perhaps we have opened an arena for discussion that may consolidate Graslund's theories.

Interestingly, the Chapel Stile frieze faces the 'reborn' sun in the east and is close to a river into which cremated remains may have been placed (eventually entering the sea via Lake Windermere).

Rock art in the open landscape is invariably located within the hill country of Northern England and southern Scotland, often close to the sources of streams and rivers. The 'language' of these sites is incredibly consistent, as described and interpreted above, with some local variation. Open-landscape rock art is probably the result of a Neolithic association with the 'life-giving' and 'life-sustaining' elements of rainfall and water-flow, and with the transfer of the sun's energy in the form of light and warmth.

Our research suggests that calendar stones were time-keeping devices requiring regular observations of the cycles and phases of the sun and moon. Linear grooves, or 'pointers', appear to direct the onlooker's vision towards key calendrical events on a distant skyline, such as the solstices and equinoctial sunrise and sunset. 'Counters' are the domino stones or Moon-phase calculators (see above), and probably used observations of the moon to subdivide the year into *approximately* twelve months, or the synodic month (of 29.5 days) into four lunar weeks, each of seven or eight days. These stones are fundamentally different in character to the vast majority of open-landscape rock art; they were created for a specific purpose. The domino stones probably had their origins within the Neolithic (see chapter eight), whereas the linear pointers, being less weathered and uncompromisingly imposed on rock surfaces (unlike the Neolithic open-landscape tradition), probably date from the Early Bronze Age.

Although confident in our rock art interpretations, some motifs may have more than one meaning or purpose. Apart from its prime utility purpose, the Neolithic stone axe may also have been a symbol of power, a form of currency, a gift or a funerary deposit. It may have possessed magical properties. But at the end of the day it was still a stone

Fig. 38. Cups within a 'boat' shape.

axe, albeit beautifully crafted. Similar attributes may have been given to rock art. There are several motifs the purpose or meaning of which we can only suggest, and others that we simply do not understand.

It is rare to find more than a single cup within a ring. Again on Brow Moor, we have an example of a 'boat-shaped' enclosure containing seventeen or eighteen cups of varying size, deeply pecked into the flat top surface of a rock (fig. 38). Could each cup have been recording the years of the lunar Metonic cycle, which takes 18.6 years from major standstill to major standstill? If we bear in mind that the moon rises close to the maximum southerly standstill point on the horizon over a period of about eighteen months, and that the authors observed this event in 2005 only after consulting *sky-map.org*, prehistoric observers could be forgiven for failing to be absolutely accurate. It is also probable that these people had quite short life expectancies, meaning that unless the task of recording was passed down through the generations, a single observer may have only experienced the major lunar standstill on two occasions. Our observation of this event was made by sighting along a nearby cup-marked 'pointer' stone, located only 300 metres to the south-east (Smith and Walker 2008, 82). Furthermore, is it beyond the parameters of possibility that, if seen as a counting device, the same arrangement may have doubled not only for counting years within the Metonic cycle but also for counting lunar months over the major standstill period? Eighteen cups could have sufficed for either or both.

Alternatively, if we consider the cups not as 'counters', but as souls, or people (see above), then are we looking at a representation, perhaps of an extended family, actually travelling in a seagoing boat? Perhaps this was the means by which a group of people arrived here. Or was this motif a stone-carved record of a distant folk memory? The sea is visible from this stone. Again, could this idea have been incorporated as part of a time-flow reference to the Metonic cycle of the moon, using a boat to symbolise the passage through time? As we have come to realise in earlier chapters, the Neolithic people were knowledgeable and sophisticated, making economic use of natural resources, particularly within the present North York Moors – that is, statements in stone that probably functioned at several levels of understanding.

Many motifs on the North York Moors still remain a complete mystery to the authors. Wild guesswork as to their meaning or purpose would be pointless and would probably undermine our credibility, which is built on careful observation and reasoned argument.

MARK-MAKING ON STONE SURFACES

There is evidence, based on observations made on Brow Moor, that rock motifs were initially plotted using arrangements of pecked dots. Taking a closer look at the 'boat-shaped' enclosure (see above), it is apparent that the bow of the 'boat' was not completed but had been delineated by a series of circular indentations (fig. 39).

Nearby, in the Astro-Geometric Zone, are two earthfast stones described in chapter seven, both showing small dots in their surfaces. The Cross Stone has a straight row of fine peckmarks alongside the southern end of the north–south linear arm of the cross motif. It is only visible under strong, low sunlight (fig. 40). In chapter seven we argued that this row could have been an early attempt at the north–south line, later revised, implying that accurately locating the cardinal directions was of vital importance to the artist (see pages 55–6).

A few paces away, the Hugh Kendall Stone has two circular indentations that, in combination with a single cup, create an alignment to the north (fig. 41).

Visible from the Hugh Kendall Stone, also on Brow Moor, is a cairn that we investigated in relation to this stone in chapter seven. A ring of upright slabs lies within the body of the monument.

An excavation in 2004 of 10 per cent of the monument revealed extraordinary motifs on one of the stone slabs, since identified as Slab 1. Very fine circular pecked dots appear to be defining two lines that were either never completed or were ignored in the final development of the design. Coupled with chiselled grooves of a very sharp and precise nature, it does seem that stone tools would have been inadequate in the creation of such marks. The authors believe that fine-pointed and chisel-edged tools were therefore made of metal. Clearly, this would date Slab 1 and its containing monument to the Early Bronze Age (fig. 42).

The precise and 'imposed' nature of the previously mentioned Cross Stone and Hugh Kendall Stone leads us to believe that these motifs also belong to the Early Bronze Age.

Associated with the Brow Moor Monument, an egg-shaped sandstone cobble (a possible 'baetyl') was discovered on the old ground surface immediately east of the cairn.

Fig. 39. Circular indentations apparently delineating the bow of boat-shaped enclosure.

Fig. 40. Cross Stone, showing row of peck marks.

Left: Fig. 41. The Hugh Kendall Stone.

Below: Fig. 42. Slab 1 of the Brow Moor Monument shows two arrangements of finely pecked dots.

1. *Above and above left:* Cups, rings, basins and flow channels: all birth symbols, implying the veneration of streams and rivers. *Left and below left:* Spiral motifs: entry into the Realm of the Dead. *Below:* The River Coquet 'dies' in the salty, tidal lower reaches at Morwick.

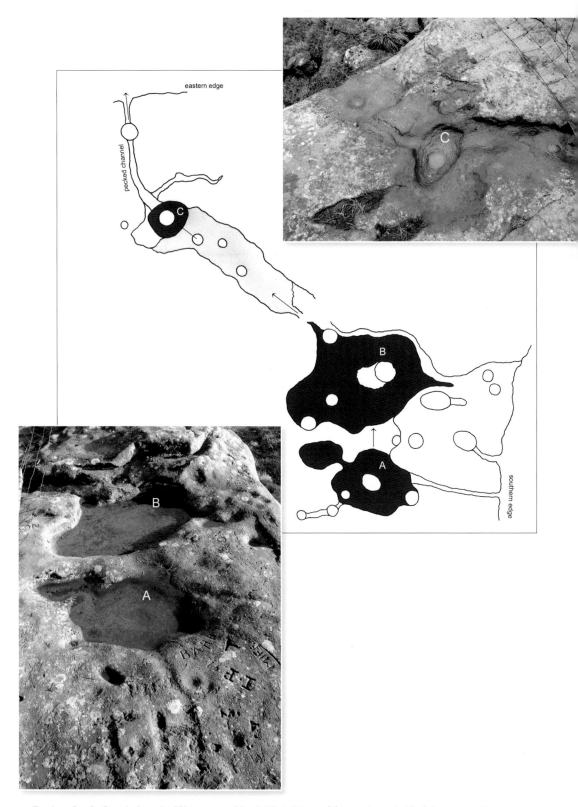

2. Rock 1, Garfit Gap, below the Wainstones, North York Moors. The southern half of the top surface area illustrates how 'basins' and channels have been modified in order to create water-flow features. They are punctuated by countersunk cups. Arrows indicate the direction of flow. Both photographs look towards the east. (The plan drawing was produced by Paul Brown from rubbings made at the site.)

3. Two stones with cups and flow channels at Allan Tofts, North York Moors.

4. Rock sculpture at Old Bewick, Northumberland.

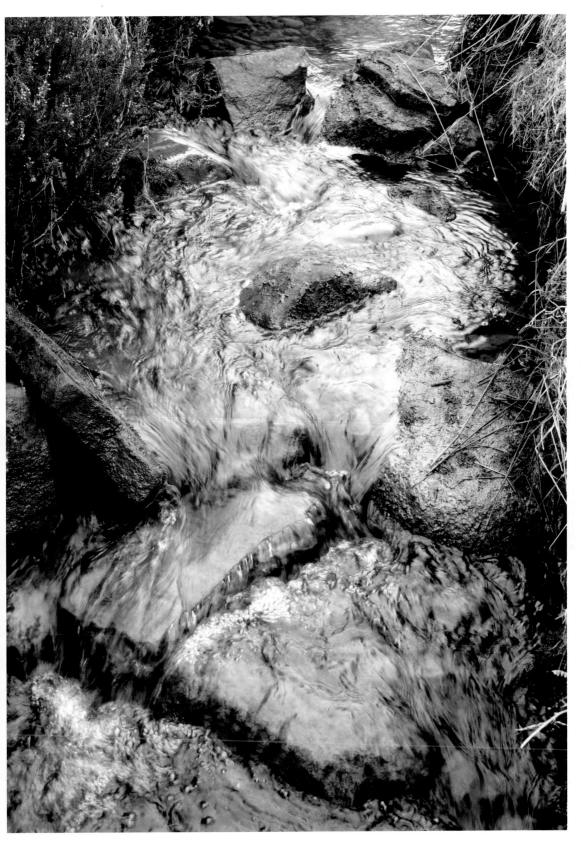

5. A fast-flowing hill stream.

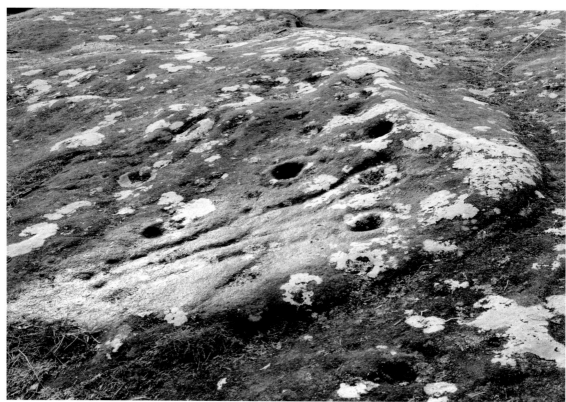

6. Flow motifs at Roughting Linn, Northumberland.

7. *Above and inset, clockwise:* Midsummer sunrise. Newgrange baetyls, symbols of birth/rebirth, face the east. A cup-and-ring motif with a south-facing groove draws in the sun's energy to its central cup or 'soul'. *Below and inset:* Sunset: entry into the Realm of the Dead. Slab 1, Brow Moor Cairn.

8. A Mayan pyramid at Chichen Itza, Yucatán, Mexico. (*Simon Byers*)

9. *Above:* A simulation showing Orion due south above the Castlerigg portals at midwinter. *Right:* The constellation of Orion.

Betelgeuse

Bellatrix

Orion's Belt

Salph

Rigel

10. Funeral pyres beside the River Bagmati, Kathmandu, Nepal, in 2008. (*Ken Grant*)

11. Basins and channel at Lordenshaw, Northumberland.

12. Rock sculture at Lordenshaw, Northumberland. Note the the twelve-cup domino stone on the left.

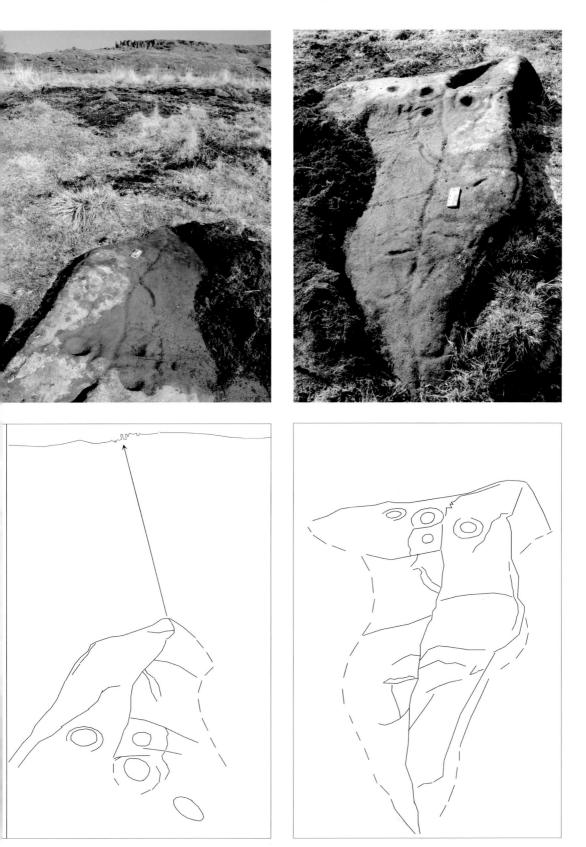

13. Rock 7, Garfit Gap, points toward the Wainstones and displays a grid design.

14. Seeds and sweets discovered in rock motifs at Roughting Linn, Northumberland.

15. Carved and painted Mani stones in Nepal in 2010. Note the small pebble offerings in niches within the stones. (*Ken Grant*)

16. Showery Tor, Bodmin Moor.

Fig. 43. An incised and peckmarked baetyl at the east of the Brow Moor Monument.

This 'portable' stone had precise incised linear and angular pecked markings that could have been created with the same metal tool(s) as was used to create Slab 1 (fig. 43). The significance of this rounded, marked stone has been indicated earlier in this chapter and in chapter seven.

The vast majority of rock motifs on the North York Moors and throughout the British Isles are believed to belong to the Neolithic – the New Stone Age. Metal tools were not available during this period. In the third chapter of our first volume of *Rock Art and Ritual*, we wrote:

> Deer antlers are remarkably sharp and resilient and come with ready-made handles. Our experiments on sandstone (well away from rock art sites) show a capability to accurately peck out a design into the virgin surface of a rock, but probably not to create the deep recesses associated with completed rock motifs. (Smith and Walker, 2008)

After describing the discovery of an unusual flint artefact in an area of Brow Moor with concentrations of rock art, we continued:

> Is it just possible that the Brow Moor flint could have been fashioned with rock art in mind? Placed into peck-marks and the hollows of cups within recognised rock art on Brow Moor,

this flint proved to be a remarkably close fit. The sturdy tip is capable of pecking or being driven into sandstone with applied pressure in a twisting motion, like a bradawl. The sharp edge immediately below the tip has just the right amount of curvature for the function of scouring out a cup, the very area on the flint with smoothing on the surface and horizontal scratching. (Ibid.)

Millstone grit is coarser than sandstone bedrock (favoured for creating rock art), and is therefore another strong candidate for deepening and smoothing motifs. Even during the Early Bronze Age, stone tools would still have been the norm, with bronze probably limited to people of high status for the production of tools and weapons.

REFERENCES

Beckensall, S., *Prehistoric Rock Art in Cumbria* (Stroud: Tempus, 2002).

Burl, A., *The Stone Circles of the British Isles* (Yale University Press, 1979).

Burl, A., *Great Stone Circles* (Yale University Press, 1999).

Graslund, B., *Prehistoric Soul Beliefs in Northern Europe* (Uppsala University Press, 1994).

Smith, B. A., and A. A. Walker, *Rock Art and Ritual: Interpreting the Prehistoric Landscapes of the North York Moors* (Stroud: Tempus, 2008).

Tilley, C., *Metaphor and Material Culture* (Oxford: Blackwell, 1999).

Walker, A. A., and B. A. Smith, 'By the Waters of Ravenscar' in *British Archaeology* 89 (York: CBA, 2006).

10

Mind-Maps and Ritualised Landscapes

In chapter one, we briefly looked at some of the problems involved in open-sea navigation during the Neolithic, and how these may have been addressed:

- By following a coastline or heading towards visible land.
- By recognising landmarks.
- By recognising wildlife.
- By establishing north–south coordinates.
- With 'mind-maps' recalled from memory, then passed on verbally. (There is no evidence for the physical creation of maps. Such organic materials as wood, leather or fabric would have had little chance of surviving into the twenty-first century.)

Many of the same principles established for seagoing navigation could have been applied to direction-finding (orienteering) on land.

Natural linear features within the landscape – such as coastlines, streams, rivers, valleys and ridges – must have been of paramount importance. Such features remain very much the same today as they were during the Neolithic, a major difference being the change in vegetation and land use. Natural forest or woodland that occupied much of the lower-lying land in valleys or plains has largely been replaced by cultivated fields or human settlements. The remnants of glacial lakes and overflow channels may now only be seen as boggy, poorly drained land. The moor tops and the high ridges in particular provide wide vistas (unless commercially forested), enabling other hills to be seen and recognised. During the Neolithic, the tops appear to have had patchy, thin tree cover, and the process of deforestation had begun. Similar distant views are therefore possible from the highest ground (Innes 2008, 149).

Landmarks, seen as major points of reference, must have included hills, especially those with unusual or dramatic appearance, just as headlands, rock outcrops and offshore islands would have been recognised and used as navigational aids by seafarers. Two such hills (known as outliers) at the northern extremes of the North York Moors must have been those now known as Roseberry Topping and Freebrough Hill. Others may have included the 'twin peaks' of Easterside and Hawnby Hill, Whorl Hill, and, to the south-east, Blakey Topping and the intervisible Howden Hill. In chapter six we established that Neolithic people had a highly developed sense of shape and form.

Fig. 44. An incised line to Freebrough.

In giving directions for overland travel, the shapes of the hills mentioned above (and doubtless others) could have been scratched into earth or stone or other surfaces – each has distinctive characteristics. If indications were then made in directional terms (i.e. lines), then we would be considering a rudimentary map. But no such 'maps' have been positively identified, certainly none that have been scratched into earth. There may be some evidence, however, that direction lines towards these hill landmarks were incised into stone (fig. 44), or were indicated by deliberate alignments of burial mounds during the Early Bronze Age (Smith and Walker 2008, 120–2).

Early Bronze Age burial mounds were constructed in two rows on moorland between Roseberry and Freebrough. Such alignments may have been in recognition of the 'sacred' quality of these two hills (ibid. 125). The more northerly row has an almost exact east–west orientation, and the tumuli are fairly evenly spaced along the OS grid line NZ 127. This points to recognition during the prehistoric that the two hills, 11 km apart, were fortuitously located along a major east–west cardinal, and emphasises an ability to accurately establish a cardinal line, even though the two hills, in this instance, are not intervisible. This ability would have been vital to prehistoric orienteering.

In chapter seven we demonstrated that north–south cardinals could easily have been established using a gnomon and measuring the length of the shadows cast by the sun. The shortest shadow, at midday local time, points directly north. Several examples of linear grooves pecked into stone on Brow Moor, probably during the Early Bronze Age, remain as testimony to the prehistoric ability to establish not only north–south cardinals, but also the east and west. Three stone circles in Cumbria (see chapter seven) belonging to the Neolithic period also demonstrate an ability to achieve accurate alignments to the north–south and east–west cardinals, emphasised in the choice of size or shape of standing stone. Swinside has a tall, tapering stone at the north and a large, square stone at the south. Long Meg's circle has huge blocks at the east and west. Castlerigg has two sets of portals at the north and south.

Prehistoric travellers crossing the North York Moors would probably not have had the luxury of time to spend in measuring shadows. Approximate bearings relating to the east, south and west could have been established by watching the position of sunrise, guessing midday when the sun is highest, and noting where the sun was setting. They would have had a good idea of the time of year by the length of day and the height of the sun, and they would have been able to 'fine tune' observations made of the sun with additional knowledge of the seasonal patterns displayed by flora and fauna. Such an ability to use the sun as a form of compass may have been second nature to prehistoric travellers – an instinctive sixth sense. This ability is now possibly lost to 'civilised' travellers in the high-tech world of the twenty-first century; we are dependent on compasses and satellite navigation systems. Did we once have a similar ability to the homing pigeon? A friend, Richie Wiberg, recently achieved first prize with his pigeon in a racing competition from Lerwick, in the Shetland Islands. His pigeon travelled a distance of 391 miles to Teesside, North East England, and averaged 53 mph, making the journey in less than 7.4 hours. It still remains a mystery as to how these birds navigate and return to their home lofts after such extensive journeys with such accuracy. Suggestions include using the sun as a compass, or having highly sensitive natural magnetic sensors 'wired' into the brain. Even

Fig. 45. Richie and his prize-winning pigeon.

so, after travelling in a basket (and therefore deprived of any directional clues), how does a bird know which way to travel on being released? Like human travellers, pigeons do follow the coast on such lengthy journeys – and even motorways.

Should the sun have been hidden by cloud cover, prehistoric travellers may have resorted to natural indicators in order to establish the approximate direction of north. For example, because the sun never enters this region of the sky, dampness may remain on the northern faces of rocks or trees. Mosses and other water-loving vegetation often colonise such places, providing a green 'colour-coded' guide for travellers as a consequence. Similarly, patches of snow often remain on the northern slopes of hills, rocks and gullies long after the sun has melted the rest. Once again, we see that precipitation and the rays of the sun are inextricably linked as part of the prehistoric cosmic equation.

As with the authors' personal experience, repeated moorland crossings over many years would have enabled our prehistoric travellers to construct a detailed map of the moors within the mind. This would have included memories of important landmarks such as hills with distinctive shapes (see above), crossing points of streams, areas to avoid such as bogs or dangerous cliffs, and certain stones (marked, unmarked or standing). This remembered information could be considered a mind-map, details of which could be shared verbally, by making arm and hand gestures, or by scribing into the earth. Tracks and pathways were probably kept open by repeated use, either locally or on long-distance routes, the former frequently punctuated by small cairns, the latter by Early Bronze Age burial mounds, often along the high ridges. Tried and tested over generations, such trails must have represented the safest routes, as well as taking lines that avoided boggy areas and steep climbs as much as possible.

Long-distance walkers on the North York Moors still use ancient waymarkers, be they the shapes of distinctive hills or valleys, standing stones, or prominent burial mounds. OS maps are studded with such reference points along ancient routes. Furthermore, these features all have names. Some of these names may have filtered down from prehistoric times. Here is a short list of names from the gruelling 42-mile Lyke Wake Walk, from Osmotherly in the west to Ravenscar on the east coast, using the highest points in the moorland landscape:

- Scarth Nick (glacial overflow channel)
- Scugdale
- Live Moor
- Cringle Moor
- Cold Moor
- Wainstones (spectacular natural rock outcrop)
- Urra Moor
- Round Hill (highest point on the North York Moors, surmounted by an Early Bronze Age burial mound)
- Face Stone (waymarker of unknown date with deeply engraved face)
- Esklets (the source of the River Esk)
- Margery Bradley (Neolithic standing stone, a waymarker)
- Flat Howe
- Loose Howe
- Shunner Howe
- Wheeldale Howe
- Blue Man-i-th'-Moss (Neolithic standing stone, a waymarker)
- Simon Howe
- Eller Beck
- Lilla Howe
- Jugger Howe
- Stony Marl Howes
- Beacon Howes

By giving names to features within the landscape, ancient travellers were making what could frequently be a hostile environment more familiar – in twenty-first-century jargon, more 'user-friendly'. Such names would have been another means of passing on information relating to travel verbally, in the same way that we use modern landmarks such as church towers, pubs and other distinctive buildings when giving directions. Explaining distances between landmarks may have been achieved in terms of time – half a morning in summer, a full morning in winter, for example. The ability to establish approximate cardinal points, or to distinguish between left, right and straight ahead, would also have been essential, both as a mental structural framework for a mind-map, and as a means of disseminating directional information.

RITUALISED LANDSCAPES

That areas of landscape became ritualised during prehistory is certain. Features such as rock outcrops, isolated hills, dips in the hills (known as cols), the banks of rivers and elevated areas around the sources of water typically attracted attention. These became special, even sacred, places. Rock art or monuments (especially funerary monuments) within, or relating to, such features are to be found throughout the British Isles.

In our first volume of *Rock Art and Ritual*, we suggest that Garfit Gap at the north-west of the North York Moors had been adopted in its entirety for ritual purposes:

> Is it possible that a small, perhaps semi-nomadic population, mainly occupying the fringes of the North York Moors during the Neolithic period, adopted a minimalist, energy saving policy with regard to ritual within the landscape? Why not use features already present in the landscape in their totality? Why drag megalithic stones over many miles of difficult terrain and risk being crushed in the task of raising them, when natural pillars of megalithic size already stood impressively against the sky? Why create an avenue, causeway or cursus, when a natural beheaded valley, lined with stones, ready for marking, could be used as a ritual route-way? Instead of erecting stone entrance portals to direct passage into such a ritual pathway, two large, natural, earthfast boulders, with just the right amount of space to pass between them, could be utilised and serve the same purpose, saving many man-hours of hard physical work. Of course, the 'ready made' ritual landscape suggested above is the Wainstones/Garfit Gap area, the subject of this paper.

Another example in the same region is Brow Moor, the most elevated land on the east coast south of the Firth of Forth. Here, the authors rediscovered a network of lost pathways by plotting the positions of rock art and apparently associated small cairns. Distribution patterns strongly suggest trails around the moorland that avoided such obstacles as steep climbs, boggy areas and watercourses where possible. At eight locations, cup-marked stones have been found *within* watercourses at probable crossing points (Walker and Smith 2006, 46–7). This area has numerous Early Bronze Age burial mounds, at least one 'observatory', and the greatest concentration of rock art on the North York Moors.

Enigmatic stone rows, pit alignments and linearly arranged post holes are to be found throughout the British Isles from Cornwall to Mid Clyth in northern Scotland. Some may have had astronomical or calendrical functions, while others appear to direct the viewer towards rock outcrops or distant hills, or to form links between watercourses and a variety of monuments. Some may have been 'processional' ways. Earthen banks and ditches crossing the landscape appear to have fulfilled similar functions, frequently isolating the ends of spurs on the North York Moors for probable ritual purposes.

On Bodmin Moor, Cornwall, there are many stone rows. A detailed appraisal of this specific ritualised landscape is to be found in chapter eleven.

'Avenues' of stones often link stone circles and other monuments with streams or rivers. We cite Aubrey Burl in *The Stone Circles of the British Isles*:

> Four miles east by the Kennet, probably in Broadstone West Meadows, eight huge stones stood in a wrecked circle of which Stukeley wrote, 'over against Clatford at a flexure in the river, we met with several great stones'. These had gone by 1890, including four that may have formed a short avenue down to the river. (Burl 1979, 317)

The massive henge and stone circles at Avebury once had an impressive avenue, the Kennet Avenue. Burl again:

> Despite being of stone instead of earth the Kennet Avenue has a similarity to the avenue at Stonehenge and it may be wondered if, like that, it was not a later addition to its circle-henge. Both lines have an end near the major river of the region, both are associated with beaker pottery, and both led to a concentric circle, the Sanctuary and the Stonehenge bluestones. By coincidence, their lengths are comparable, one and a half and one and three-quarter miles respectively. (Ibid. 327)

It is of interest to note that funerary burials and deposits have been found against some of the Kennet Avenue stones. These are rarely on the eastern side, but frequently on the west. This phenomenon compliments our observations in chapter seven, and the association between death and the sun setting in the west.

We return to the North York Moors, and Skelderskew Moor near Commondale. We find a stone row and earthwork apparently linking the head of a small stream in North Ings Slack with an area of marshy headwaters at Tidkinhowe Slack to the north (NZ 607066). The stone row crosses a watershed. Within 100 metres of the stone row, a group of Early Bronze Age burial mounds, of which Hob-on-the-Hill is the most prominent, lies on raised ground to the east. Was the stone row and bank a link between the sources of water and the funerary site? In chapter four, we argued that water sources might have been associated not only with the birth of a stream, but, symbolically, with birth in general. If this was so, then do we once again see evidence for belief in the rebirth of the souls of the deceased? The Hob-on-the-Hill funerary site also lies to the east of the stone row, which, by coincidence or by design, is on the side of the rising sun, another rebirth symbol (fig. 46).

Could it be that the stone row was an attempt to symbolically 'hard-wire', or tap into, the energy of two life sources at the north and south? In 1991, a limited excavation was

undertaken by Vyner and Sherlock to investigate the structure of the monument. They discovered that the stone orthostats predate the earthen bank, which later encapsulated the middle section of the stone row. Was this to consolidate Early Bronze Age beliefs and the purpose of the monument (Vyner 1995, 27)?

We mentioned above that the sunrise was a symbol for rebirth. It can hardly be fortuitous that the Hob-on-the-Hill tumulus lies on the sight line of a large, badly damaged cairn on a summit at NZ 634 123 in the west. The same line leads towards Freebrough, a probable sacred hill in the east. This sight line also passes between the two Black Howes, as if they were portals framing the summit of Freebrough. Was this another symbolic energy line, directed not only towards a probable sacred hill but also towards the 'reborn' sun in the east? We must stress at this point that we are not talking about 'ley lines' (fig. 47).

So far under the heading 'Ritualised Landscapes', we have discussed monuments that are, or were, clearly visible in the landscape. Some alignments, however, may have been *invisible* to the 'uninitiated'.

Earlier mention was made of a west–east alignment of Early Bronze Age burial mounds just to the north of that described above. This arrangement is more precise and appears to link two 'sacred hills', Roseberry Topping in the west and Freebrough Hill in the east. Of course, the almost exact west–east configuration of these two hills is entirely fortuitous. Evenly spaced over 11 km, the alignment of cairns and tumuli appears to represent a form of celebration of this knowledge. This apparent alignment is even more remarkable because the two hills are *not* intervisible.

In Garfit Gap, at the north-west fringes of the North York Moors, large rocks with markings form a huge crescent when plotted onto an OS map. All of these rocks appear to use the dramatic rock outcrop known as the Wainstones as a backdrop, suggesting that it may have been of ritual importance and a focus for activities below. In 2009, after reading about this site in chapter five of our first volume of *Rock Art and Ritual*, Colin Keighley discovered another large rock to the south, at the eastern fringe of the site. This had cups with single rings and several linear grooves. Paul Brown, author of *Prehistoric Rock Art in the North York Moors* (2005), was informed of the discovery. Brown visited the site and found two further rocks near to Keighley's, and another near a public footpath further south on the western side of Garfit Gap.

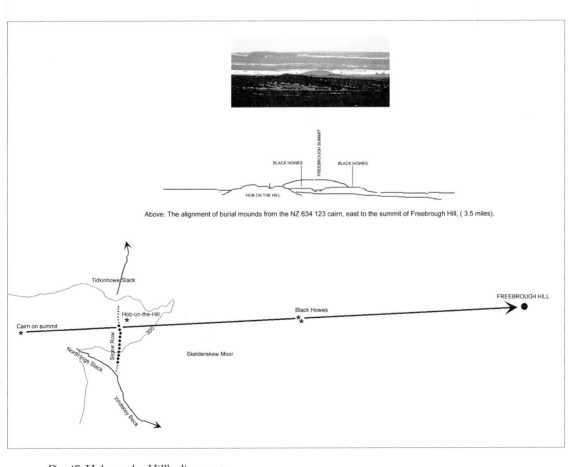

Above: The alignment of burial mounds from the NZ 634 123 cairn, east to the summit of Freebrough Hill, (3.5 miles).

Fig. 47. Hob-on-the-Hill's alignments.

Visiting the site in 2010, we located all four rocks. Once again, the Wainstones were spectacularly visible from all of them. On plotting their positions onto an OS map, it became immediately apparent that three of the recent finds, plus R4, a 'Grid Stone' with cup and triple rings discovered by Smith, were exactly aligned on the Wainstones, very close to true north! This was a distance of over 900 metres. Furthermore, the cluster of three is central in this alignment, and the Grid Stone is midway between the cluster and the Wainstones. Are we looking at a planned arrangement, as opposed to pure coincidence? If planned, this alignment would have been invisible to the 'uninitiated' and very difficult to organise and create (fig. 48).

Interestingly, R4 and R9 (our reference numbers) lie beside old pathways that lead into Garfit Gap. It is entirely possible that a lower-level pathway above a ravine also passed close to the three-stone cluster R7, R8a and R8b. This might suggest a further dimension to the rock art alignment. Such stones could also have functioned as symbolic 'gateways' into a special place that lay to the north-west of an 'invisible' demarcation line (fig. 49).

Of particular interest is Rock 7. Earthfast, this rock tapers to a point that appears to be directed towards the Wainstones outcrop. Additional emphasis is given to this direction by the creation of a pecked groove running centrally down this rock, culminating in a final shift that precisely aligns with the distant outcrop on the skyline (col. pl. 13). Furthermore, grooves running both perpendicular and parallel to this directional emphasis create a 'grid' pattern. In chapter nine, we expressed our opinion that the grid designs are found at 'entry points' to special (sacred?) places with a proliferation of rock art beyond. Bearing in mind that this rock and Rock 4 were probably beside ancient trails leading into Garfit Gap, we may have both a 'pointer' to the Wainstones and a 'gateway' into Garfit Gap expressed within a single carved rock (col. pl. 13).

The above observations and findings surely defy the laws of chance. Looking again at the plan of rock art distribution in Garfit Gap (fig. 48), our suggestion is compounded by yet another apparent alignment a few degrees east of true north through rocks 3, 2 and 1. If this line is extended, it aligns with Roseberry Topping, 6 miles to the north (currently hidden by a forestry plantation), even though the latter is not directly visible from rocks 3 and 2. Along with the Wainstones outcrop, Roseberry is very dramatic in appearance on the skyline, and both may have been considered as deities during prehistory (fig. 50). The observer, even if ignorant of the recent changes in the appearance of Roseberry, would probably consider that the close to true-north alignment of rocks 3, 2 and 1 was targeted at this hill.

Looking at the photograph and the apparently aligned rocks, it appears that the near-true-north line misses the summit of Roseberry (fig. 50), connecting instead with the western shoulder of the hill. In 1912, the south-west face of Roseberry collapsed in dramatic fashion, due to mining activities below. This means that the summit was earlier situated further west (as viewed from Cold Moor). If we consider that further collapses have quite possibly occurred over a period of 5,000 years, since the middle Neolithic, such an alignment may well have been directed towards the summit at that time.

The pagan Anglo-Saxons gave the name of one of their greatest and most popular gods to this dramatic-looking hill. Roseberry Topping is derived (via a complicated

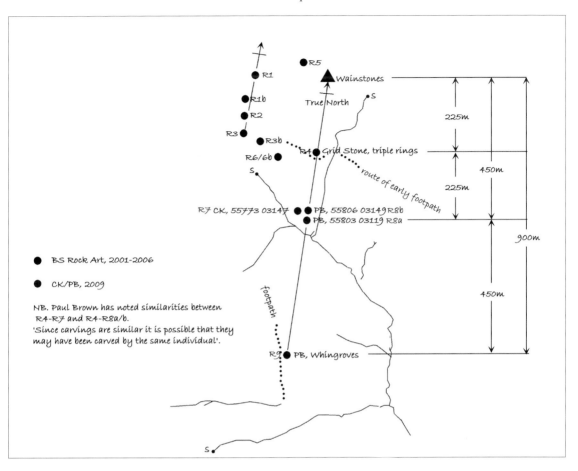

Fig. 48. Rock art in Garfit Gap shows the 'Crescent' and two apparent alignments, one to Roseberry Topping 6 miles to the north, and one to the Wainstones (see fig. 50, overleaf).

Fig. 49. Garfit Gap to the north-west. The sight lines are close to true north and the routes of two footpaths towards the Wainstones from marked rocks.

Fig. 50. A near-true-north alignment through rocks 3, 2 and 1 towards Roseberry from Cold Moor.

linguistic route) from 'Othensburg' or 'Odin's Hill'. Woden was the same god. It is possible that the Wainstones is a colloquial abbreviation of 'Woden's Stones'. Here the god dwelt, in the minds of people 1,500 years ago. Were these hills endowed with sacred attributes 5,000 years ago, in the minds of Neolithic inhabitants? Perhaps they were seen as the link between the earth and the sky, the upper layers of their cosmos?

Before leaving Garfit Gap and two apparent alignments of rock art with what are possibly sacred prehistoric hills, yet another factor appears to consolidate Neolithic intentions. All of the rocks in both alignments (including Rock 7 as part of the three-stone cluster) have a variety of **complex motifs**, including cup clusters, cups with rings, domino cups, oval shapes, grids, other linear grooves and water features. Apart from Rock 5, the Snake Stone, actually outside of Garfit Gap, and Rock 1b (which is closely associated by proximity and similarity of features with Rock 1), the few other known rocks boast only simple cups or basins. Extensive searches have revealed nothing definite elsewhere. As things stand, it would appear, by the exclusivity of their selection for carving complex rock art, emphasis was given to stones aligned on either the Wainstones or Roseberry Topping. Also, and incredibly, both alignments are to true north, or very nearly.

FURTHER POSSIBILITIES

In 2004, the massive rock outcrop of Roughting Linn in Northumberland was visited. Instead of the rock art being picked out by water-flow or sunlight (see chapter five), the recessed motifs were filled with either seeds or 'dolly mixture' sweets in a variety of colours (col. pl. 14). Whether the work of children or adults, such non-destructive twenty-first-century enhancement may have taken place, perhaps as a fertility ritual, in prehistory. Of course, sweets would not have been used, but quite possibly seeds, which were surely as symbolic as the baetyl stone 'eggs' of birth or rebirth (see chapter nine). Similarly, different varieties (and colours) of berries may also have been chosen. The link with the birth of a stream and the final destination of a river, the sea, may have been marked by sand, small multicoloured pebbles, and seashells. Pigment, such as ochre or chalk or the juice of certain berries, could also have been applied. Judging by the depth of some rock carvings, the motifs may well have undergone re-scouring at regular intervals. We can only suggest such ritual practices as a possibility. In *Viking Age Sculpture*, Richard Bailey states under the heading 'Appearances Deceive: Polychrome Carvings':

> We have seen that the chances of survival may mislead the modern scholar. But even when a stone *has* survived its present appearance can be deceptive, because we have good evidence that many, if not most, pre-Norman sculptures were originally painted.
>
> We know that paint was used on English stone carvings before the Viking settlements: eighth and ninth-century sculptures at Monkwearmouth *TW* and Ilkley *YW* still carry traces of a red colouring, and both blue and black can be seen on the runic stone from Urswick *Cu.* (Bailey 1980, 25)

Rock art beside established trails might have been the prehistoric equivalent of present-day shrines (col. pl. 15) – maintained for travellers or local people who, in passing these stones, could make small ritual deposits in the carvings. Deposited 'gifts' of many kinds, even today, are often placed into hollows in stones, no doubt with good-luck wishes. The tops of several orthostats mentioned earlier in the Skelderskew Moor stone row are severely weathered. In the deep recesses, hill walkers frequently deposit coins. A hollow in the top of Ralph's Cross, which stands beside the road on Blakey Rigg high on the North York Moors, used to contain coins left by travellers. Wild flowers, small food offerings, even photographs of loved ones, are a common occurrence in shrines throughout the world.

During the Bronze Age, votive offerings of deliberately damaged metal objects, often of considerable value, have been found deposited in pools of water at many locations. Similar wishes for improvements in life probably accompanied such acts of ritual.

Perhaps in looking at rock art today, what we are seeing may be the bare bones of something far richer that existed during prehistory. Over the millennia, any evidence of such activities suggested above would surely have been lost, but this is no reason to doubt their existence. Such ritual practices would, in any case, have been of a transitory nature, the rain and wind constantly cleansing these hill-country rocks to leave a fresh 'canvas' for a new day. This could be likened to the building of sandcastles on the beach, like making footprints in fresh snow, or indeed the brief passage of a human life within the greater scheme of things.

REFERENCES

Bailey, R. N., *Viking Age Sculpture* (London: Collins, 1980).

Brown, P., and G. Chappell, *Prehistoric Rock Art in the North York Moors* (Stroud: Tempus, 2005).

Burl, A., *The Stone Circles of the British Isles* (Yale University Press, 1979).

Innes, J. B., 'Appendix 1: Northern North York Moors Vegetation History to the Middle Bronze Age' in *Rock Art and Ritual: Interpreting the Prehistoric Landscapes of the North York Moors*, B. A. Smith and A. A. Walker (Stroud: Tempus, 2008).

Walker, A. A., and B. A. Smith, 'By the Waters of Ravenscar' in *British Archaeology* 89 (York: CBA, 2006).

Conclusion to Part Three

In both chapters nine and ten, emphasis is given to the importance of the location of rock art within the open landscape. It would appear that, along with the surfaces selected for carving, such considerations were of equal importance to the nature of the carvings themselves during the Neolithic. Rock art associated with funerary monuments was fundamentally different.

Discoveries within former ritualised landscapes of the North York Moors are uniquely those of the authors (see chapter ten). They are the result of years of observing, careful recording and the precise plotting of data onto OS maps. We are always seeking to reveal distribution patterns within the landscape that may tell us more about the behaviour of prehistoric inhabitants.

On elevated ground at the extreme east of the North York Moors, above Robin Hood's Bay, a moor fire in 2003 gave us the opportunity to locate and plot the ground positions of all the rock art revealed by the fire. The end result was the rediscovery of a network of lost prehistoric pathways.

The apparent alignments of either orthostatic stones or tumuli during the Early Bronze Age on Skelderskew Moor, and on moorland between Roseberry Topping and Freebrough Hill (just to the north), are remarkable. The west–east alignments of tumuli are repeated, and defy the laws of chance.

Furthermore, in Garfit Gap, during the Neolithic, large earthfast rocks were apparently selected exclusively for carving with complex motifs (especially cups with rings). Were they identified during prehistory as being orientated virtually true north–south within two separate alignments, or is this pure coincidence? Add to this the fact that both alignments appear to be focused on probable 'sacred' hills or outcrops, and we have something approaching a revelation regarding insights into the workings of the prehistoric mind – its ingenuity and its cosmos.

The prehistoric inhabitants of the North York Moors were intelligent, sophisticated and resourceful. They demonstrated deep reverence for the landscapes they lived in, and into which they wished to make permanent ties via rock art and the construction of monuments. The phenomena of alignments and the veneration of various landforms within the landscape are not, however, confined to the North York Moors. In part four, other landscapes are considered, landscapes that became ritualised in similar ways in places as distant as Southern England and the Orkney Islands, beyond the northern extremities of the Scottish mainland. Examples from other parts of the world, thousands of miles apart, suggest a universal desire to connect with the landscape and with the heavens, including in this century.

PART FOUR

CHALICES OF THE ANCESTORS – FURTHER REFLECTIONS

(Based on research conducted by
Alan A. Walker over a number of years.)

Introduction to Part Four

Water flows, it is living, it moves: it inspires, it heals, it prophesies. (Eliade 1958, 200)

The fact that water is both a fundamental component of, and essential to, all life on Earth needs no further elucidation. This considered, our detachment from nature within modern western society has largely reduced this most precious liquid to its utilitarian value. It is piped into and out of our buildings. Agencies and contractors facilitate supply. We turn a tap and out it flows, as we continue our complex and competitive lives. It is only during flood, drought or when we encounter water within the landscape that we may give it a second thought. Perhaps a waterfall, a moorland stream, a mighty river or a magnificent lake may inspire, as indeed they have for poets and artists since time immemorial.

Students of religion have long understood the spiritual significance of water to early societies. It figures in creation myths worldwide and is usually a significant factor in the establishment of universal order, sometimes being the primordial element itself. Water was used in rituals involving purification and regeneration and it is there, at the bitter end, in all destruction myths.

More recently, anthropology has shown that water still carries some of these and other values within globally diverse groups that may be considered to be more 'in tune' with nature than modern western society.

In part four we explore the apparent association between a variety of watery contexts and examples of Neolithic and Early Bronze Age monuments in Britain and Ireland. We consider these as part of a broader package reflecting the importance of water within (at least) local cosmologies and suggest that water has significantly influenced certain aspects of rock art in the open landscape created at that time.

Firstly, however, we want to relate a personal experience recorded in Alan's diary.

13 JULY 2003

I had waited patiently for months for the opportunity to revisit a spectacular carved stone that, due to a combination of deeply carved depressions and channels, I had dubbed 'the Basin Stone' when I had first stumbled across it in the late winter of

Fig. 51. The Howdale Basin Stone.

2002. With the advent of spring, and with it the breeding season for grouse and other ground-nesting birds, forays onto sensitive moorland had been suspended to minimise impact on a fragile ecosystem. The heart of Howdale Moor, where the Basin Stone lies (NZ 95861 01522), was unmanaged moor hosting a plethora of flora and fauna within and around a broad basin, which is the remnant of a former glacier-dammed lake and is still fed by the rainwater run-off from Brow and Howdale moors. This, other carved stones and a small cairn are located on a tongue of elevated ground that is situated between two intermittent watercourses. An earthwork (a water-channel) associated with the eighteenth-century alum industry had been created to divert water at the head of this tongue of land. Prior to this interference, this raised area would have become an island during and after inclement weather.

With every mile driven from Scarborough on 13 July, the weather deteriorated. Entering the car park situated opposite a radio mast (indicating the end of the gruelling 42-mile Lyke Wake Walk that crosses the North York Moors from west to east), 266 m above sea level, low cloud clung to the moor and rain felt imminent. Undaunted by climatic conditions that could be described, at best, as atmospheric, Bruce (my canine shadow) and I left the security of the car and set out into the mist. After a strenuous

20-minute trudge through deep heather and hidden rivulets, we arrived at our goal, just as steady rain started to fall. The mist rapidly closed in to create a microcosm enveloping human, canine and Basin Stone, isolating them from the outside world. Regaining composure, I removed my rucksack and reached for my camera.

The light conditions were totally inadequate for photography, and in any event, 'still' photography could never have captured the dynamics of the event that I was now witnessing. The rain had filled the carved depressions that cover much of the stone's surface and as more rain fell, water was actually flowing from and between the carved motifs. The cups, channels and basins had 'come to life'. Rain fell, water flowed and time was lost.

Bruce barked. The light was fading and darkness hastened. Now soaked to the skin, I grabbed my rucksack, glanced briefly once more at the stone, and, not daring to linger, followed Bruce into the mist and safely back to the car as darkness fell.

Driving home through the rain, I realised that the channels linking the cups and basins were not simply decorative. They must have been intended (during rainfall) to control the flow of water into and around other carved hollows within this stone. At some time in prehistory, such rock sculptures (and their latent meaning) must have been of sufficient importance to be given the necessary investment of time, energy and skill in the process of their creation (fig. 51).

11

Water and the Neolithic –
The Cornish Connection

Alan visited Cornwall's Bodmin Moor, Roughtor to be exact, while on holiday in the summer of 2004. Ascending the uppermost granite slabs, camera around his shoulder, and nearing the Logan Stone balanced at the summit, it would seem inconceivable that basins, artificial or natural, could occur in such hard rock. There were no handholds or footholds, no indentations. All was rounded in this most elevated and exposed place, presumably the result of millions of years of harsh erosion. To Alan's amazement, at the summit and invisible from below, were several rounded basins, water-filled, rippling in the breeze and glistening below the surface. He looked for signs of carving and peckmarks. None were to be found. The hollows seemed almost too perfect, but there they were. The very purpose of the climb – to photograph the surrounding landscape, which is peppered with Bronze Age hut circles and field systems – was forgotten. The basins were strangely compelling. Then, just for a moment, the wind dropped, and he saw his reflection in the level water. He remembered that night in July last year, the 13th, water and stone... But Alan was certainly not the first to be seduced.

'OF THE ROCK BASONS...'

> In Cornwall there are Monuments of a very singular kind, which have hitherto escaped
> the notice of Travellers; and, though elsewhere in Britain, doubtless, as well as here, in like
> situations have never been remarked upon (as far as I can learn) by any Writer; they are
> Hollows, or artificial Basons, sunk into the surface of the Rocks. (Borlase 1769, 240)

The above quotation is from a most remarkable volume, *Antiquities Historical and Monumental of the County of Cornwall*. Its researcher and author, William Borlase (1696–1772), was initially educated in Penzance and Plymouth and later followed his father's footsteps by taking Holy Orders shortly after graduating from Exeter College, Oxford. Borlase resided for 50 years at Lugdvan near Penzance, where he guided the spirituality of his parishioners. During this half-century of devotion to his 'flock', family and garden, he occupied his spare time by studying and recording the antiquities and natural history of Cornwall.

The first edition of *Antiquities* was published in 1754, with an expanded and updated second edition just three years prior to his death. Despite severe criticism of his views pertaining to druidism – an obsession he shared with his contemporary William Stukeley – the volume remains immensely important as it recorded very accurately and with acute observation many monuments and landscapes, some of which have since have been damaged or lost.

The opening quotation introduces a chapter where Borlase describes and interprets the rock (or solution) basins found on the granite tors of Cornwall. We briefly summarise: he proposed that the basins were made by druids to collect undefiled rainwater for ritual purpose. The argument was made first by dismissing all possible practical uses, then by drawing on classical and biblical sources to qualify the sanctity of pure water. Borlase ably applied his hypothesis to the Nuevo Druidical movement of his time. It was unfortunate that he could not have known at that time that the basins are entirely natural, their inception probably around 40 million years ago, in a warmer climate. In mid-eighteenth-century Europe, many scholars supported the argument of the seventeenth-century cleric Archbishop Ussher, who had calculated within a biblical timescale the Earth's creation to 4004 BC. Hence there was no concept at that time of prehistory, and gradualist geology, the foundation for modern geology, was yet unfounded. We may forgive William Borlase his indiscretion. The basins do, to the casual observer, look manmade. Some remarkably so.

Since 2004, Alan and his family have returned to Cornwall on four occasions. Each visit has included at least two days trekking to and climbing tors, searching for basins that show signs of human modification. None have been found to date; all so far examined seem to be entirely natural. However, there are in some instances clear relationships between tors where the exposed granite has solution basins and monument construction. Archaeologists Barbara Bender, Sue Hamilton and Chris Tilley (all of University College London) were probably the first to make this connection, during a recent large-scale multidisciplinary archaeology project examining Neolithic and Bronze Age landscapes on Bodmin Moor. They published some of their findings in *Stone Worlds* (Bender et al 2007). Despite Leskernick, a small hill to the north of moor, being the main focus for survey and excavation, the team considered it worthwhile to visit all the moor's tors and record the presence, or otherwise, of solution basins. They qualify that 'the fantastic scalloped profiles' can be found on twenty-one of the thirty-six principle hills of Bodmin Moor and although it does not always follow that major outcrops on prominent hills will have basins, they are absent on hills without significant outcrops (ibid. 432). The basins are not exclusive to Bodmin Moor; they are present, for example, above Zennor in West Penwith, at Carn Brae Hill near Redruth, and on the Isles of Scilly.

The apparent relationship between some of these basins and Neolithic monuments is noted and will be discussed and expanded upon below. The UCL team also acknowledges that at least part of William Borlase's interpretation may hold water:

> Shorn of the references to Druids and the idea that these basins were carved by people, Borlase's interpretations of the potential symbolic significance and use of the solution basins seem very plausible. Indeed, the prehistoric populations may have shared Borlase's view that they were carved, but by ancestral rather than human beings. The use in libations and ceremonies of the purest water of all, that which falls from the sky, seems entirely credible. (Ibid. 434)

Fig. 52. Recumbent human being in tor basin.

So, with this belated exoneration of at least part of William Borlase's hypothesis, it will be useful to briefly discuss the phenomenon of solution basins before exploring how they fit into a much broader context, which we will argue reflected a fundamental part of ideology within our Neolithic.

Basins are probably best described as rounded or oval indentations in the upper surfaces of stone slabs, the result of deep weathering. Gradually, the hollows increase in size as the matrix of the granite degrades. They are most often located on the uppermost granite slabs of tor outcrops, however, it does not follow that the most exposed stone would necessarily have most basins. The basins are not visible from the ground. They vary considerably in size, from a few centimetres to a metre in diameter, and some have the depth of a shallow bath. The bottoms of the hollows tend to be flattish and it is common to find a bed of quartz crystals at the base, deposited during the degradation of the granite. Some have an outlet or outlets on their perimeters, allowing water to discharge when the basin is full. As Borlase noted, these have no directional bias. He, however, proposed that this was deliberately arranged, to allow the most convenient point of collection for the water into a vessel placed below (Borlase 1769, 255).

Sometimes the granite between juxtaposed basins will degrade, creating most unusual shapes. For example, at King Arthur's Bed on eastern Bodmin Moor, a series of basins have joined to form the shape (and size) of a recumbent human being (fig. 52).

Occasionally, basins wear completely through the slab to form a hole.

What William Borlase observed was entirely the result of natural forces, created over an almost inconceivable period of time.

MONUMENTS, SETTLEMENT AND BASINS

An interesting addendum to the *Stone Worlds* publication, table 19.1 (Bender et al 2007, 436), lists the thirty-six hills and tors of Bodmin Moor, their heights and the types of outcrops and numbers of solution basins on the main stacks. Although, as noted above, the UCL team has touched on an apparent association between basins and Neolithic monuments, we thought it may be interesting to look at data on all the hills and tors to see if any patterns emerged.

To establish a method, however crude due to lack of excavation, the possible destruction of sites by industrial processes, and data missing for other reasons, we divided the monuments and settlements into periods as safe as we considered possible. Firstly, the Neolithic, which included long cairns (Johnson 1994, 26; Herring and Rose 2001, 14), a henge (Herring and Rose 2001, 23) and two defended enclosures tentatively ascribed to the period (Johnson 1994, 48). Secondly is a category that includes monuments that could date from the later Neolithic but probably date from the Early Bronze Age. These included stone rows, settings and circles (Herring and Rose 2001, 17) and simple, kerbed and ring cairns. About 400 such cairns have been recorded on Bodmin Moor (Herring and Rose 2001, 19), and nine radiocarbon samples suggest that the principle phase of cairn building on the moor was about 2150–1750 BC (Christie 1988, 164). Our three categories were therefore Neolithic sites, late Neolithic/Early Bronze Age sites, and finally those with no apparent association from either period. Each category was then subdivided into those with and those without basins. We also looked at the relationships with topographic features such as watercourses or the tallest peaks.

The late Neolithic/Early Bronze Age monuments were found to be present on the majority of the thirty-six hills and tors, irrespective of the presence or absence of solution basins. It is also interesting to note that monuments from this period, in particular cairns, stone settings and circles, are to be found in abundance in totally unrelated geographical contexts (Barnatt 1982; Bonney 1994, Map 1; Johnson 1994). Although Bender et al clearly consider an 'unequivocal' relationship between ritual monuments and solution basins was present at that time and cite four examples (Bender et al 2007 434), it is clear that by then, this was not the only factor influencing the location of monument construction. These instances may best be considered remnants of the continuance of an earlier tradition, or simply fortuitous.

If, as we propose, during the Early Bronze Age the basins lost their earlier significance, this may echo the demise of open-landscape rock art within other regions during that period. It is well attested (see citations in Vyner 2007, 102–7) that earlier carved stones were broken off, and that crude emulations of Neolithic carvings were hurriedly made for inclusion in some Early Bronze Age funerary monuments. It is broadly accepted that the production of open-landscape rock art ceased during this period, perhaps coinciding with the inception of land division and the intensification of agriculture.

It is worth sidetracking to briefly consider that stones in these instances are only 'visible' to archaeologists due to the presence of symbols. The stone itself would have carried metaphysical value to the builder or the interned, most probably both. It is entirely feasible that other unworked (and as such unrecognised) lithic material, possibly with provenance from important landscape contexts, was placed within such monuments (see Pollard and Gillings 2009). This was certainly the case at Malton Cote Farm, Scamridge, North Yorkshire, where large quantities of non-local stone were imported for inclusion within a large burial mound. Today, the mound is almost entirely destroyed by ploughing, but considerable quantities of the exotic stone can be observed on the top of, and next to, the locally sourced dry-stone field walls in the immediate vicinity of the monument's site.

When the Neolithic sites are considered, it is apparent that on Bodmin Moor at least, all these have association with solution basins. It is also interesting to note that in geographically local tor groups, such as Bearah–Kilmar–Trewortha, Catshole–Tolborough–Butters and Roughtor–Brown Willy, **the Neolithic activity has not necessarily been focused on the most elevated hill, but upon the one with most basins**.

Of the few hills and tors without ritual-related monuments from either period, roughly half have basins. Some, such as Kilmar and Trewortha, which have fifteen each, may, as noted above, have been ignored during the Neolithic because nearby Bearah, with even more, carried the greater significance within that locality. The same circumstances may have prevailed but for differing reasons in the Early Bronze Age. At this time it is likely that a hill that was to become the focus for a ritual monument would probably relate to a nearby settlement, such as at Leskernick Hill, where a substantial cairn was built at the beacon. It is worth noting that Herring and Rose (2001, 19) have suggested that such hilltop cairns may have been regarded as artificial tors. Two stone circles and a row were also built nearby, to the south-east of the settlement. As well as convenience, it is likely that other factors influenced their location. High Moor and Codda Tor were slightly further away from the Leskernick settlement and to reach them would have involved crossing wet areas, hence they were apparently ignored. It seems that by the Early Bronze Age, various factors, including demography, geography, and celestial alignments, came into play, influencing the location of ritual-related monuments (or the lack of them).

To return to the apparent association between the basins and Neolithic monuments and enclosures, Bender et al (2007, 434) have established relationships between the Bearah Tor long cairn (SX 2630 7433) and the Louden long cairn (SX 1401 8032) and rock stacks that have basins. They also note that the Trevethy Quoit, situated at St Cleer, roughly 4 km south of Stowe's Hill (see right), has a massive capstone over its forecourt, with a weathered-through solution basin. The nearest granite outcrops with basins are at Stowes Hill. The selection and transportation of the slab must, therefore, have been deliberate. Its removal from a sacred landscape and the act of transportation would have carried powerful symbolism (fig. 53).

Further, they suggest similar circumstances regarding Clitters Cairn (SX 2414 7821), where a substantial, and apparently imported, granite slab with three basins is located directly adjacent to the cairn. Although the authors describe the cairn as of Bronze Age origin, this is not clear. Excavation by Brisbane and Clews (1979) has shown that the cairn predates the field system within which it is located and, as such, it may be from an earlier date than anticipated.

The only other long cairn currently recorded on Bodmin Moor, at Catshole Tor (SX 1714 7828), also has an association with basins. It is interesting to note that nearby Codda

Fig. 53. The Trevethy Quoit.

Tor has more extensive rock outcrops than Catshole, but has no basins, and adjacent Tolborough Tor is of roughly equal elevation with exposed granite, but again without any basins. In short, **the presence of solution basins at Catshole has most probably influenced the location for the cairn**.

The two defended enclosures noted above are Stowes Pound (SX 2577 7260) and Roughtor Hillfort (SX 147 808). The word 'defended' implies protection against violence and this may be partially substantiated by archaeological evidence from a similar hilltop enclosure to which the above have been compared (Johnson 1994, 48), Carn Brea near Redruth. Here distinctive Hembury pottery, evidence of lean-to structures with occupation and industrial debris, and a single radiocarbon date of 3940–3704 BC (Mercer 2001) clearly attest to early Neolithic activity. This is supplemented by lithic evidence, notably over 700 leaf arrowheads scattered around a gateway on the east summit. Signs here of extensive burning in the same area may support, in this instance, the idea of defence against extreme violence. However, Stowes Pound, Roughtor and others remote to Bodmin Moor, such as the Neolithic enclosure at Helman Tor, have produced no such evidence. At Roughtor, the casual and intermittent nature of the ramparts and walls to the north and south sides and their total absence to the west (Johnson 1994) suggest that these were not intended for protection against intruders. It seems more probable that in the Neolithic they were intended to dominate the horizon and impress from without, and to define a ritually charged area within. The fact that later cairns and hut platforms are present inside these areas reflects a continuity of place that can be noted throughout this landscape and far beyond. During the Neolithic, before formal land division, it seems far more likely that a smaller population would have found habitation in less extreme altitudes and weather conditions. In short, we want to suggest that these elevated enclosures were at that time sacred to the living; they were the realms of the ancestors.

BETWEEN THE LIVING AND THE DEAD

Mike Parker Pearson of the University of Sheffield has argued convincingly that parts of the Wessex landscape to the west of the Neolithic monuments at Stonehenge and Avebury were considered liminal, and may have represented 'domains of the ancestors'. The monuments themselves represented transitional points between realms of the living and those of the dead (Parker Pearson 2000), an idea originally published by the Madagascan archaeologist Ramilisonina (1998a, 1998b).

The roots of his hypothesis lie in an ethnographic analogy with the dominant cultural group in Madagascar. The Merina, a society of over a million people of Southeast Asian origin, have been the focus of comprehensive study by anthropologist Maurice Bloch (1971, 1982, 1989 and 1992). Their complex funerary ritual includes the exhumation of the dead as a transitional process before their inclusion in massive megalithic tombs in the traditional homeland. This is central to a belief system where fertility is absolutely dependent upon ritual associated with the ancestors. To the Merina, the merging of the ancestors, their ancestral lands and the living is considered an ideal. The blessing of the ancestors is conveyed to the living via a ritual involving water that has been stored for a year or so within the ancestral tomb, and is thereby imbibed with the potency of the ancestors. The gifts of children, wealth, crops and strength were, and are, dependent on the blessing.

> It is the power of total enablement to total achievement. Without blessing, a person is impotent in all senses of the word. (Bloch 1982, 212)

The act of blessing survives into the Christian era.

The key issue here is the association of the ancestors, water and fertility, and their interdependency relating to continuity and socio-religious order. Were the Merina an isolated ethnographic paradigm that could be conveniently used to help elucidate aspects of our prehistory, the argument that water is a key element in superstition and religious thought could probably be dismissed as fortuitous. However, for the Ancient Greeks and more recently the Zuni Indians of North America, the Desana of South America, and certain aboriginal and South Sea traditions (to cite just a few widespread examples), water, mythologies and cosmology are inextricably linked. This was most probably so on a much wider basis throughout the past. It is interesting to note that the figure ã not only meant water to Ancient Sumerians, but also represented sperm, conception and generation.

Returning to Wessex, Parker Pearson has built on the ethnographic foundation by drawing on the distribution of wood and stone monuments within the landscape and, interestingly, dichotomies in the spatial distribution of faunal and ceramic types within these. Briefly, he proposes that during at least part of the Neolithic, stone carried a metaphorical association with ancestors. He cited the deposition of ancestral bones in rock shelters, the greater-than-utilitarian value of stone axes and stone temper in Peterborough Ware – a pottery often found in close association with Neolithic funerary monuments (Parker Pearson 2000, 208). Peterborough Ware had a temporal overlap of several centuries with another ceramic style, Grooved Ware (Garwood 1999, 159), which was never stone-tempered. Cattle were thought to dominate the regional economy of the earlier Neolithic and pigs later, as woodland regenerated (Thomas 1999, 26). It is of interest to note that recent analysis of faunal assemblages has shown Peterborough Ware to have predominance with cattle remains and Grooved Ware with pig (Parker Pearson 2000, 209). As the two styles are very rarely found in the same context, it seems probable that they served differing purposes. Parker Pearson (2000, 204) has noted that in the Stonehenge and Avebury landscapes, Peterborough Ware and cattle remains have been found in association with stone funerary-related monuments. Grooved Ware and pig are found, sometimes in considerable quantity, at complexes with wooden structures or settings that were associated with ritual and feasting for the living, 'from whence the dead departed on their journey through the afterlife into ancestor hood' (ibid.).

We have drawn on this well-researched and documented dichotomy of constructed ancestral domains separate to, and remote from, the landscapes of the living in order to emphasise our argument regarding the potential natural liminality of the high tors of Bodmin Moor. Those with basins, in particular, were probably thought to have been created by the ancestors, or even by divine beings (col. pl. 16).

It seems unlikely that a formalised belief system was widespread during our Neolithic. It is, however, probable that there may have been regional variants on themes with similar components or comparable structures. We propose key elements were present and these were connected with water, sunlight and fertility.

Fertility, however, is also linked with death and regeneration (Eliade 1958, 352; Bloch and Parry 1982), and it is apparent that there is an association between Neolithic monuments related to funerary ritual and water and sunlight. Some of these also have rock art and, in instances, votive deposits of pottery that share similar iconography. We have argued throughout this volume that open-landscape rock art has a relationship with water-flow and the sun, although the symbolism is very different with regard to monumental rock art. We have no detailed chronology for open-landscape rock art, but in some instances we do for the monumental art and ceramics. We also have contextual information and probable uses for the monuments. With this we will consider the differences between the art forms.

REFERENCES

Barnatt, J., *Prehistoric Cornwall: The Ceremonial Monuments* (Wellingborough: Turnstone, 1982).

Bender, B., S. Hamilton, and C. Tilley, *Stone Worlds: Narrative and Reflexivity in Landscape Archaeology* (Walnut Creek CA: Left Coast Press, 2007).

Bloch, M., *Placing the Dead: Tombs, Ancestral Villages and Kinship Organisation in Madagascar* (London: Seminar Press, 1971).

Bloch, M., 'Death, Women and Power' in *Death and the Regeneration of Life*, ed. M. Bloch and J. Parry, pp. 211–30, (Cambridge University Press, 1982).

Bloch, M., *Ritual, History and Power: Selected Papers in Anthropology* (London: Athlone Press, 1989).

Bloch, M., *Prey into Hunter: The Politics of Religious Experience* (Cambridge University Press, 1992).

Bonney, D., Map 1 in *Bodmin Moor: An Archaeological Survey, Volume 1: The Human Landscape to c. 1800*, ed. D. Bonney, pp. 24–76 (London: English Heritage, 1994).

Borlase, W., *Antiquities Historical and Monumental of the County of Cornwall* (London: Bowyer & Nichols, 1769).

Brisbane, M., and S. Clews, 'The East Moor Systems, Altarnun and North Hill, Bodmin Moor' in *Cornish Archaeology* 18, pp. 33–56 (1979).

Christie, P. M., 'A Barrow Cemetery on Davidstow Moor, Cornwall: Wartime Excavations by C. K. Andrew' in *Cornish Archaeology* 26, pp. 27–169 (1988).

Eliade, M., *Patterns in Comparative Religion* (New York: Sheed and Ward, 1958).

Garwood, P., 'Grooved Ware in Southern Britain: Chronology and Interpretation' in *Grooved Ware in Britain and Ireland*, ed. R. Cleal and A. MacSween, pp. 145–176 (Oxford: Oxbow, 1999).

Herring, P., and P. Rose, *Bodmin Moor's Archaeological Heritage* (Cornwall County Council, 2001).

Johnson, N., 'The Prehistoric Landscape' in *Bodmin Moor: An Archaeological Survey, Volume 1: The Human Landscape to c. 1800*, ed. D. Bonney, pp. 24–76 (London: English Heritage, 1994).

Mercer, R. J., 'Excavations at Carn Brea, Illogan, Cornwall' in *Cornish Archaeology* 20, pp. 1–204 (1981).

Parker Pearson, M., and Ramilisonina, 'Stonehenge for the Ancestors: The Stones Pass On the Message' in *Antiquity* 72, pp. 308–26 (1998a).

Parker Pearson, M., and Ramilisonina, 'Stonehenge for the Ancestors: Part Two' in *Antiquity* 72, pp. 855–6 (1998b).

Parker Pearson, M., 'Ancestors, Bones and Stones in Neolithic and Early Bronze Age Britain and Ireland' in *Neolithic Orkney in Its European Context*, ed. A. Ritchie (Cambridge: McDonald Institute for Archaeological Research, 2000).

Pollard, J., and M. Gillings, 'The World of the Grey Wethers' in *Materialitas: Working Stone, Carving Identity*, ed. B. O'Connor, G. Cooney, and J. Chapman, pp. 29–41 (Prehistoric Society, 2009).

Thomas, J., *Understanding the Neolithic* (London: Routledge, 1999).

Vyner, B., 'Rock-Art in Cleveland and North-East Yorkshire: Contexts and Chronology' in *Art as Metaphor: The Prehistoric Rock-Art of Britain*, ed. A. Mazel, G. Nash, and C. Waddington, pp. 91–110 (Oxford: Archaeopress, 2007).

12

Circles, Lines and Water

Professor Richard Bradley of the University of Reading has shown how the monumental architecture of the British Neolithic has been influenced by cosmology. The earliest of these were long barrows – communal burial mounds that Bradley (1998) considers reflect the Neolithic long houses of the living – and the roughly circular earthworks termed causewayed enclosures, which are thought to have been meeting places for communal activities involving disparate groups (see Oswald et al 2001). The important point is the introduction of the circle into monumentality; it was later to develop into more complex structures, such as henges and possibly stone and timber circles. The latter, with the exception of rare examples preserved by saturated conditions such as Seahenge (Bradley 2007, 123), only survive as staining where they have decayed in the ground; they are called post pipes by archaeologists. Notable examples are at Durrington Walls and Woodhenge to the east of Stonehenge, both of which Parker Pearson associates with ritual connected with funerary practices (see above). Henges and stone circles enjoy a much better survival rate above the natural ground surface. Many are damaged, some have been romantically restored, and many more sites, particularly henges, await discovery, perhaps during construction projects. Henges are approximately circular earthworks, generally with an outer bank and inner ditch. They vary tremendously in size and have one or more entrances. Clearly their morphology discounts any defensive qualities. Detritus, evidence of burning, and internal settings and structures suggest that mass activities, including feasting, took place within. Like the stone and wood circles, they are considered ritual-related monuments. Stone and timber circles are sometimes found in association with henges, as noted above and at Avebury. Stonehenge, however, is atypical and must be considered on its own merit.

Generally, however, it is accepted that henges and stone circles are regional variants of a similar class of monument. Aubrey Burl (2000) has demonstrated that the circles tend to be sited on upland areas with thinner soils where stone is available; earthwork henges occupy less elevated landscapes with deeper soil and without suitable stone. Both were in use from about the middle of the Neolithic, although it is unclear when they fell into disuse. Some endured into the Early Bronze Age.

Bearing in mind that people at these times would surely have exploited all terrains, Burl's hypothesis seems at first consideration to make sense. It is reasonable to assume that by the middle of the Neolithic the lowland areas would have supported the greater

Fig. 54. A 'modest' stone circle, Wayworth Moor, North York Moors. The view is to the west.

populations. The sheer number of henges already documented (and those that known distribution patterns suggest remain to be found) seems to support this hypothesis. Henges separated those within from the landscape outside, creating a microcosm with a false horizon. They are often located in geographical basins, and many enjoy close spatial relationships with running water. They are also found in close association with another, more enigmatic, type of Neolithic monument, the cursus, to which we will return shortly.

Stone circles rarely have any of these qualities. Many of the upland circles are modest features that could have been raised by a small workforce with moderate expenditure of time and effort (fig. 54). Even if the gaps were filled with screens between the stones, the people inside would in most instances have been able to see out to, and connect with, surrounding elevated landscapes (see also chapter six).

We want to now reconsider if circles and henges were really serving exactly the same function, and then to question how the communities that built them disposed with the majority of their dead. Could these factors assist with our understanding of open-air rock art created within upland landscapes?

Archaeologist Dr Jan Harding of Newcastle University has noted that the design of henges

emphasised a concern with the renewal or reproduction of the world, their circular shape drawing on the cyclical movement of celestial phenomena. Further, the symbolism and experience of these monuments created a sense of stability and changelessness: for to enter these sacred arenas was to become at one with the timeless forces that controlled the cycle of birth, death and rebirth. The potency of the association provided the monuments with a long-term continuity in their design. They were to endure over 500 years. (Harding 2003, 54)

It is interesting that the circle and concentric circles are recurrent symbols in British and Irish open-air rock art and much further afield. We have shown that in many instances within the local landscapes we have surveyed, the stones selected for carving with complex symbols have been chosen due to their orientation and angle to the sun. In low light, shadows are cast within the pecked and incised motifs, creating emphasis, possibly even suggesting that the grooves are wet. We consider the circular carvings to be far more complex than simply representations of the sun (Anati 1964, 47), a matter to which we will return (see also chapters four and nine).

Harding also considers that the distribution of henges in relation to water may also offer useful insights to their purpose:

A concern with fertility, reproduction and renewal may account for another distinctive characteristic of the monuments … water represents a fundamental element in many non-Western societies. It guarantees the fecundity of people, animals and plants, and as noted, rain is often regarded as the seed of a Sky Father. There is nothing more essential to living than water, yet its unpredictability and unbridled power can be a harbinger of suffering and even death. The flow of water is also a potent metaphor for movement or journeys, and it is commonly linked with social notions of purity and pollution. It is therefore more than possible that later Neolithic religion associated areas of water, such as rivers, springs and bogs with supernatural spirits, or even with a god-like being. (Harding 2003, 55)

This quotation refers to monuments that are predominantly of the later Neolithic. We wish to qualify that these ideas did not originate at that time. Dr Harding is discussing a representation of what were already ancient ideas. By the later Neolithic it is entirely possible that the concept of gods and goddesses had developed within a religious structure, termed by psychologist and researcher of primitive religion Bruce Lerro as 'secondary magic' (2000, fig. 4.1). Before the development of complex horticulture Lerro considers that earth spirits, totems and ancestor spirits would have presided over the land. But even then, the basic concept linking water and life would have been the same. The concept of God was introduced to the horticultural Merina by Christian missionaries in the nineteenth century, however the traditional belief of ancestors conveying the blessing of fertility through water was all-important even in the twentieth century.

The association of water and henges is considerably more complex than their proximal relationship. Professor Colin Richards (1996) has observed that it is very probable that some henge ditches were deliberately waterlogged, such as at the Stones of Stenness and the Ring of Brodgar on Orkney, where two juxtaposed henges, each situated on an opposing narrow isthmus, project into lochs Harray and Stenness. Richards considers these to represent microcosms of the surrounding landscape and, as such, they are a metaphor for the builders' cosmos. Considered as an isolated paradigm, this may seem fanciful, however it is interesting to note that, as argued by Anthony Harding (2000) and observed by the current authors, henges often enjoy an obvious reciprocity with their geographical surroundings. This aphorism may well be considered a leitmotif of Neolithic ritual monuments. Perhaps at that time a major characteristic of monumental construction was the attempt to bridge the conceptual divide between the cultural and natural worlds.

We will now examine another type of Neolithic monument referred to above as the 'cursus', a term based without foundation in an antiquarian interpretation by William Stukeley (1740, 41), meaning a course or a racing track 'suitable for the racing of chariots, by the Ancient Britons'.

These enigmatic linear enclosures are generally comprised of shallow parallel ditches with inner banks, and usually with closed terminals. Well over 150 such monuments are acknowledged in Britain and Ireland. Although length always exceeds width and usually by many times, there are huge variations in size between individual monuments. For example, compare the 119 m-long cursus at Barnock to one of almost 10 km at Cranbourne Chase. North Stoke's cursus is 11 m wide, Stonehenge's is 128 m. One thing that all cursuses have in common is that, despite a considerable corpus of recent interest, no one has established their exact purpose. It is, however, apparent that, like henges, they often had spatial relationships with rivers, and in particular the confluences of these. As Dr Roy Loveday notes (2006, 134), 'These places carry cross cultural sacred significance and have always been considered communication hubs.'

At Rudston on the Yorkshire Wolds, four such cursus monuments focus on a 90-degree bend in the Gypsey Race stream, the only flowing water in the Great Wolds Valley. The two major monuments link the stream at the bend where it turns towards its death in the North Sea, near the long barrow cemeteries. Archaeologist Dr Kenneth Brophy sees many common features between rivers and cursus monuments, and considers that the linear enclosures represent a cultural manifestation of real rivers and that processional activities probably took place within them (Brophy 1999, 66). This interpretation is initially hampered by the fact that cursus monuments do not have entrances or exits. The earthworks of the monuments are continuous and the terminals are closed. However, the banks and ditches are usually slight and could be easily traversed by people wishing to enter or leave. This entire closing-off of the space within would, however, have provided a symbolic barrier. The sealed conduit of space may have been intended to be separated from the surroundings to allow the living access from one area to another without spiritual contamination. This is consistent with observation by Christopher Tilley (1994, 200):

It is not unlikely that, on Cranbourne Chase, part of the narrative of the Dorset Cursus was not only linked to initiation, but also to the themes of death and the regeneration of life. It may have operated as a linear conduit through which bodies and bones were being moved between the barrows in the central part of the Chase and [the causewayed enclosure] Hambledon Hill. Bodies were perhaps being taken out of Cranbourne Chase to a death island of the setting sun beyond its margin to the west [see also Smith and Walker 2008, 103], and being allowed to decompose, with selected bones being returned to the barrows in the central ritual arena of the Chase itself. The pollution of death was thus removed and dry, clean and ritually pure bones returned.

Again, ethnographic parallels may be drawn, not only with the Merina of Madagascar but with other cultures such as Cantonese society, where the similar practice of double burials has continued for centuries. The purpose of this practice is to de-flesh and, as such, to cleanse 'death pollution' from the ancestral bones (Watson 1982, 155).

The idea that in the period following death the body, or more specifically its disjointed spirit, can cause danger to the living is cross-cultural. The idea of ghosts hanging around causing problems is hardly surprising, given that decaying flesh carries disease, and could spread illness to anyone coming into contact with the corpse. Groups to whom superstition outweighed scientific knowledge may have interpreted this as the jealousy or malevolence of the newly deceased. Careful ritual would minimise the risk involved. This is often dealt with by purification involving water, as in the case of the Bolivian Laymi among whom, despite centuries of Christian teaching, age-old rituals are still rigorously adhered to. Here, Christianity has only served to reinforce the idea of a dualistic understanding of death in the separation of the body and soul, but falls short of taking full control of the released spirit (Harris 1982, 54).

The fear of the dead, or of ghosts, is also cross-cultural, if not global (Frazer 1933, 1934, 1936; Bloch and Parry 1982; Parrinder 1987). It is and probably always was, as is attested by Sumerian and Greek mythology, believed that the spirits of the dead could not pass unaided over water. Fraser cites examples from Australia, Asia, Africa and South America. If Dr Brophy's hypothesis was correct and long enclosures or cursus monuments did represent metaphorical rivers, this could support the idea that they offered passages, through which the living could enter the realms of ancestral dead without risk of pollution or being followed back by ghosts. Again, this has been shown to be a major fear in the burial customs of widespread cultures well into our era.

Despite occupying similar geographical contexts, the cursus monuments predate henges and are often associated with Peterborough Ware pottery. Radiocarbon dates from cursus monuments and other related monuments (Barclay and Bayliss 1999, table 2.1) confirm a common temporality with these ceramics. What is striking is that the cursus – linked with the tradition of long barrows and mortuary enclosures – fell into disuse (Last 1999, 89). Henges were constructed in the same and similar geographical contexts. These are overwhelmingly associated with Grooved Ware ceramics. As already noted, unlike Peterborough Wares this tradition does not contain stone tempers. Its decoration also introduces one of the most formal and complex material languages of prehistoric Britain (Thomas 1999, 117). Aspects of this iconography are apparent in the art found at Irish passage graves that are contemporary with this tradition. Most examples of Grooved Ware have been recovered from ritual-related contexts such as pits, and are considered as votive deposits, probably associated with feasting (Cleal 1999, 5). It is interesting to note that sherds of this ceramic tradition, bearing circular and spiral motifs, were concentrated around entrances to Wyke Down, the southern circle at Durrington Walls, and the ditch terminals at Woodhenge. This iconography is entirely contextually consistent with that found carved into stone, at entrances to the Boyne Valley passage graves (Brindley 1999, 135). However, the zigzags, chevrons, lozenges and lattices that are shared by the Grooved Ware and passage grave traditions are extremely rare in open-air rock art. Single spirals are found in all three, but only in the open when

Fig. 55. Three linked spirals on a north-facing cliff above the River Coquet, Morwick, Northumberland.

associated with a ritual monument, or, in two cases, on north-facing cliffs devoid of direct sunlight overlooking the lower reaches of rivers, just before they reach the sea (fig. 55). These contexts may also represent gateways, as the fresh water will soon turn to salt as it meets what mythologies see as another realm, one considered hostile to the living – the ocean (see also chapter eight).

PASSAGE TO THE ANCESTORS

Symbols that are common to Grooved Ware have been shown by Jeremy Dronfield (1997) to have deliberate spatial distribution within Irish passage graves such as Knowth, Loughcrew and Newgrange. Some motifs occur with a major bias in certain parts of megalithic structures. These symbols are consistent with those in the abstract art of ethnographic and historic sources that had, or are known to have, cultural affinities with altered states of consciousness. Conversely, the endogenous forms of these are absent from cultures without these trends (Dronfield 1995, 539).

He has also argued that Irish passage tomb art was itself derived from endogenous visual phenomena and was associated with mind-altering practice, and that this was associated with accessing an ancestral realm through a state of intoxication and trance (Dronfield 1995, 545).

The types of images experienced during altered states of consciousness are controlled by the human nervous system. All human beings, irrespective of their cultural background, are likely to perceive images including grids, dots and spirals while entering a state of trance. This phenomenon has been extensively researched by psychologists in the twentieth century (see Pearson 2002). A little over 5,000 years ago, when Newgrange and Knowth were built, the hard-wiring of the human nervous system did not differ from that of today.

It is understood that the spiral is a key element in the process by which humans enter a state of trance, triggered by stimuli including sensory deprivation, fatigue, rhythmic movement, hyperventilation (Horowitz 1964, 512) and psychoactive agents (Barber 1970, 32). Rudgley (1998, 130) has noted that henbane, an acknowledged hallucinogen, has been identified on fragments of Grooved Ware. This may have been linked with achieving ecstatic states in ritual activities.

The carvings within the passage graves were clearly intended to be seen, but only by those allowed access with flickering torchlight, or in the case of Newgrange, only when it was illuminated briefly by sunlight through a light box strategically positioned over the monument's entrance at around the winter solstice. Flickering light is acknowledged as one of the factors that can induce a state of trance. As noted above, the very symbols carved within the monuments are those that would be experienced as phosphenes in the subject's mind's eye when entering trance. Further, recent research has shown that a sample of six chambered monuments, including Newgrange and other Irish passage graves, were all found to have primary (natural) resonance frequencies of around 110 Hz. These acoustic frequencies are known to change activity patterns in the brain's prefrontal and left temporal cortex with the precision of a switch being thrown – resulting in, according to Paul Devereux (2006, 29), the 'irruption of transient but vivid mental imagery and auditory hallucinations. It is the ideal brain frequency to be encouraged if one is conducting ritual activity.' Devereux also notes that, as a one-off, this could be passed off as an interesting coincidence (ibid.). The fact that all six sites tested demonstrated this same phenomena is remarkable, and suggests that this feature was probably an empirical discovery by the prehistoric builders and was deliberately employed in at least some of their chambered monuments.

The process by which a state of trance is entered, specifically when under the influence of certain mind-altering substances, has been shown to follow three distinct stages. During the first of these, the subject experiences entoptic phenomena such as those described above. These luminous percepts derive primarily from the human optic system and are not hallucinations. Many of the images have been noted as recurrent in Aboriginal rock art (Oster 1970, 83, 87); they also consistently feature in the monumental rock art associated with Irish passage graves. During the second stage, the brain attempts to reconcile the entoptic forms into meaningful, representational images based on cultural influences. The third and deepest stage is entered via a vortex or rotating tunnel (Horowitz 1975, 178), on the sides of which are lattices of geometric shapes from the first stage. Within the compartments of the lattice are visualised the first true hallucinations (Clottes and Lewis-Williams 1998, 17). Referring to trance and ritual within Irish passage graves, Lewis-Williams argues:

> If Neolithic people were led by belief and emotionally charged ritual to expect visions of their ancestors, the dead would very likely have appeared in the segments of the lattice that were an integral part of the vortex, through which they moved into the spiritual realm. (Dronfield 1997, 62)

In this cultural package the spiral carries powerful symbolism, both on real and metaphorical levels, and these are likely grounded in both natural and psychological phenomena. To the people who made and understood these carvings, the physical and metaphysical dichotomy that we perceive simply would not have existed. To them the symbolism was powerful and very real.

Dronfield (1997, 54) suggests that in association with Irish passage graves, the motifs represent passages to, or points of access with, other worlds, a hypothesis supported by ethnographic evidence from modern tribal societies (Ripinski-Naxon 1993, 112). Through these passages, while in ecstatic states of trance, not only was contact with the ancestors possible, but the souls of the recent dead could pass safely to the ancestral realm.

It is, however, very unfortunate that the whole trance-and-imagery phenomenon has been hijacked and linked with ideas extant in modern shamanism. In some cases they have been applied to all rock art – everywhere and from every period. We certainly disagree with any such interpretation, but do consider, in the instances discussed above, that drug-induced trance, within environments designed to encourage these experiences, was very likely to have happened and may well be responsible for some of the imagery. However, this does not mean it was shamanism. The young people that attended rave parties in the early 1990s took ecstasy and were mesmerised by repetitive sub-bass music and coordinated visuals, but they were hardly shamans. Believe it or not, they did it because they enjoyed the experience, or at least they thought they did at the time. It was to them extraordinary, and could be interpreted as a form of ritual. They were in states of trance and they had visual and auditory hallucinations, especially while in the 'rush' after taking ecstasy, which was often mixed with other drugs such as amphetamines, LSD, or almost anything else that clandestine chemists could get their hands on. It would be impossible to recreate these conditions in a laboratory.

However, the three-stage trance process has been shown in clinical experiments to be experienced by people taking LSD, and it is very interesting to briefly consider the background to this drug. It was first created as LSD-25 by Dr Albert Hofmann during medicinal research in 1938, in which he was attempting to synthesise molecules from the parasitic fungus ergot, which is found on diseased sedges and grasses, including cereals. Ergot's psychoactive alkaloids are mainly derivatives of lysergic acid, a chemical upon which LSD is based. Without entering a much deeper argument regarding monumentality, society and agriculture (see Thomas 1999, 24), it is certain that by the middle of our Neolithic, cereals were being cultivated and ergot would have been encountered. Its properties were likely to have been understood due to ingestion following the occasional contamination of cereal crops. At present, however, this conjecture has no hard evidence.

What, though, is certain is that another plant with psychoactive properties, henbane, was used in conjunction with Grooved Ware (see above). This intoxicant is known to be a powerful hallucinogen and its use as such is well attested on a geographically and temporally widespread basis (see Rudgley 1998, 127). Henbane has very similar properties to another species, datura, which has also been widely used since time immemorial in ritual (ibid., 78). It is interesting that America's rock shelters (which were occupied in prehistory) have produced botanical remains that include large quantities of datura seeds. The shelters also have direct association with panels of rock art, some images of which depict human beings associated with figures identified as the fruit of the datura.

If the people who used Grooved Ware understood the properties of henbane, it is likely that they understood those of other easily sourced hallucinogenic plants and fungi. Henbane has not been identified on earlier pottery types. The traditions of Grooved

Ware and passage graves are contemporary. The shared iconography is generally different to that found in rock art in the open landscape. These contrasts are due to alternate priorities within differing social structures and economies.

THE DEVELOPMENT OF A RITUAL LANDSCAPE

The Boyne complex in County Meath, which includes the extensively excavated and well-documented monuments of Newgrange and Knowth, has more to offer. This ritualised landscape is nestled in an area between the River Mattock and a large bend in the River Boyne. They enclose an area of about 10 km² on all but the eastern side. Most of the monuments lie in fairly close proximity to the Boyne. Grooved Ware has been associated with both Newgrange and Knowth (Cooney 2000, 18), and both are roughly contemporary with the early phases of Stonehenge and Avebury in Wessex. The chronology of most other monuments in the Boyne complex remains unclear. These include other passage graves, satellite mounds, a long mound, four henges, a timber-and-stone circle, three deliberately created ponds, and, interestingly, a cursus. The cursus and long mound are probably the earliest ritual monuments in what developed over time into a sacred landscape. Again, we see the link between natural and symbolic rivers and the ancestral dead. As noted above, in Britain the cursus tradition has an association with long mounds and causewayed enclosures and predates henges. What seems entirely clear is that the area carried great significance long before the passage graves were built. Although there is debate that some carved stones may have been reused from earlier monuments, it is clear that the contextually specific carvings on which Dronfield based his hypothesis must have been deliberately made during, or after, the construction of the passage grave. Hence they post-date the cursus and long mound by a significant period. As this symbolism is not present in the earlier monumental tradition or the associated ceramics, the art may be attributed to ideological change that inspired a new monumentality. In other words, the art developed from the ideas that reached Wessex and Ireland around the start of the third millennium BC.

The presence of manmade ponds situated close to rivers is interesting. Gabriel Cooney (2000, 166) has noted their circularity and commented that there may be a link with the henges nearby. One pond is actually two circular, conjoined ponds. He also reminds us of Colin Richards' suggestion, that flooded henge ditches in Orkney were intended to reflect the land-and-water relationships of the surrounding landscape. As this is clearly speculative, we want to suggest another possible purpose for the ponds. The water within them would have been still, or nearly so. The Boyne is a fairly fast-flowing river and has poor reflective qualities. The Mattock, a much smaller tributary, also lacks these. The fact that running water is so close discounts a practical purpose for the ponds. The passage graves include deliberate astronomical alignments (see Ruggles 1999), suggesting that celestial objects and events were of interest at (and after) the time of their construction. The calm waters of the ponds may have been associated with reflections of the night sky. A reflection, say of the Moon, captured within the water would surely have carried enormous symbolism. It could directly link the upper and lower spheres of what Randsborg has described as a vertically ordered worldview (1993, 119). Mircea Eliade describes this concept as an *axis mundi* (1964, 259). It is a point of contact between the world of the living and those of the spirits (Lewis 1986, 92).

If this was so, why had it become necessary to communicate with the spirits in such a way? Further (as convincingly argued by Dronfield), why were rituals involving induced states within elaborate monuments required for communication with the ancestors? Was this all part of the ideology that accompanied the new monuments and ceramics?

If the ancestors had once been metaphysically present within landscapes shared with the living, it seems that the new order placed the spirits of the dead into another sphere, one that may be considered exclusive and only mediated by the elite.

Returning once again to Avebury and Stonehenge, it is of note that both monuments include bank-and-ditch earthworks and stone circles, albeit in very different form. Current consensus suggests that the earthworks of both monuments were likely to have been roughly contemporary with each other and that the stone settings post-date these (Pollard and Reynolds 2002, 89). It is clear that both monuments developed through time, and the addition of the stone circles served a purpose that either refined the original monuments or had a different significance.

If both Avebury and Stonehenge were originally considered gateways from the lands of the living to the realms of the ancestors (as in the already ancient tradition that had involved causewayed enclosures and cursus monuments), did the introduction of the stone reflect an ideological refinement? Did this legitimise the potency of the monuments by reflecting the permanence of the ancestors through the medium of stone, in much the same way that we discussed in chapter eleven regarding Bodmin Moor?

This could also extend to the introduction of avenue approaches to these monuments. In both instances, these link real rivers to the monuments with carefully planned courses that serve to emphasise the phenomenological impact of the experience to the visitor. Did these avenues represent an extension of the cursus tradition as a new form of metaphorical river? Perhaps these were the appropriate routes from the flowing waters of life, which lead to the liminal and transient stations of the ancestors. In the ideology at that time, were the ancestors reaching out to the living? It is through them that territories would later be established, as a Neolithic hierarchy started to emerge with the spread of agriculture and the introduction of prestigious material culture.

Having briefly explored the idea that stone-and-earthwork avenues may represent a progression of the cursus, it is worth mentioning the stone rows of Dartmoor. These modest monuments, often lost today within heather, vary tremendously in length and have little or no significant orientation. The rows may be single, double or even treble width and often without space to walk within the stones. Their chronology is also unclear, although Aubrey Burl has speculated a temporal horizon from the end of the Neolithic into the Early Bronze Age. The point of interest is that about 80 per cent of the rows terminate at a barrow or cairn, always at the head of the row (Burl 2000, 156), half of which have associations with unimposing stone circles (ibid., 158). Does this apparent association of monument types reflect 'a locally developed expression of religious ideas held over a wide part of the country' (Quinell 1988, 7)?

If it is the case that basic foundations of belief existed on a widespread basis, possibly throughout Britain and Ireland, and that these may have endured (at least in part) through the Neolithic and into the Early Bronze Age, is it not reasonable to consider that these were expressed in ways driven by regional geographical, environmental and social conditions? In other words, diverse groups could have expressed similar ideas in the best ways they saw fit at that time and place. It is up to researchers to identify and interpret these common threads.

REFERENCES

Anati, E., *Camonica Valley* (London: Lund Humphries, 1964).

Barber, T. X., *LSD, Marihuana, Yoga and Hypnosis* (Chicago: Aldine, 1970).

Barclay, A., and A. Bayliss, 'Cursus Monuments and the Radiocarbon Problem' in *Pathways and Ceremonies: The Cursus Monuments of Britain and Ireland*, ed. A. Barclay and J. Harding, pp. 11–29 (Oxford: Oxbow, 1999).

Bloch, M., and J. Parry, *Death and the Regeneration of Life* (Cambridge University Press, 1982).

Bradley, R., *The Significance of Monuments* (London: Routledge, 1998).

Bradley, R., *The Prehistory of Britain and Ireland* (Cambridge University Press, 2007).

Brindley, A., 'Sequence and Dating in the Grooved Ware Tradition' in *Grooved Ware in Britain and Ireland*, ed. R. Cleal and A. MacSween, pp. 133–44 (Oxford: Oxbow, 1999).

Brophy, K., 'The Cursus Monuments of Scotland' in *Pathways and Ceremonies: The Cursus Monuments of Britain and Ireland*, ed. A. Barclay and J. Harding, pp. 119–29 (Oxford: Oxbow, 1999).

Burl, A., *The Stone Circles of Britain, Ireland and Brittany* (London: Yale University Press, 2000).

Cleal, R., 'Introduction: The What, Where, When and Why of Grooved Ware' in *Grooved Ware in Britain and Ireland*, ed. R. Cleal and A. MacSween, pp. 1-8 (Oxford: Oxbow, 1999).

Clottes, J., and D. Lewis-Williams, *The Shamans of Prehistory: Trance and Magic in the Painted Caves* (New York: Harry N. Abrams, 1998).

Cooney, G., *Landscapes of Neolithic Ireland* (London: Routledge, 2000).

Devereux, P., 'Ears and Years: Aspects of Acoustics and Intentionality in Antiquity' in *Archaeoacoustics*, ed. C. Scarre and G. Lawson, pp. 23–30 (Cambridge: McDonald Institute for Archaeological Research, 2006).

Dronfield, J., 'Subjective Vision and the Source of Irish Megalithic Art' in *Antiquity* 264, pp. 539–49 (1995).

Dronfield, J., 'Entering Alternative Realities: Cognition, Art and Architecture in Irish Passage-Tombs' in *Cambridge Archaeological Journal* 6.1, pp. 37–72 (1997).

Eliade, M., *Patterns in Comparative Religion* (New York: Sheed & Ward, 1958).

Eliade, M., *Shamanism: Archaic Techniques of Ecstasy* (London: Penguin, 1964).

Frazer, J. G., *The Fear of the Dead in Primitive Religion: Volume 1* (London: Macmillan & Co., 1933).

Frazer, J. G., *The Fear of the Dead in Primitive Religion: Volume 2* (London: Macmillan & Co., 1934).

Frazer, J. G., *The Fear of the Dead in Primitive Religion: Volume 3* (London: Macmillan & Co., 1936).

Harding, A., 'Henge Monuments and Landscape Features in Northern England: Monumentality and Nature' in *Neolithic Orkney in its European Context*, ed. A. Ritchie, pp. 267–74 (Cambridge: McDonald Institute for Archaeological Research, 2000).

Harding, J., *Henge Monuments of the British Isles* (Stroud: Tempus, 2003).

Harris, O., 'The Dead and the Devils among the Bolivian Laymi' in *Death and the Regeneration of Life*, ed. M. Bloch and J. Parry, pp. 45–73 (Cambridge University Press, 1982).

Horowitz, M. J., 'The Imagery of Visual Hallucinations' in *Journal of Nervous and Mental Disease* 138, pp. 513–23 (1964).

Horowitz, M. J., 'Hallucinations: An Information-Processing Approach' in *Hallucinations: Behaviour, Experience and Theory*, ed. R. K. Siegel and L. J. West, pp. 163–95 (New York: Wiley, 1975).

Last, J., 'Out of Line: Cursuses and Monument Typology in Eastern England' in *Pathways and Ceremonies: The Cursus Monuments of Britain and Ireland*, ed. A. Barclay and J. Harding, pp. 86–97 (Oxford: Oxbow, 1999).

Lerro, B., *From Earth Spirits to Sky Gods: The Socioecological Origins of Monotheism, Individualism and Hyperabstract Reasoning from the Stone Age to the Axial Iron Age* (Oxford: Lexington, 2000).

Lewis, I., *Religion in Context: Cults and Charisma* (Cambridge University Press, 1986).

Loveday, R., *Inscribed Across the Landscape: The Cursus Enigma* (Stroud: Tempus, 2006).

Oster, G., 'Phosphenes' in *Scientific American* 222, pp. 82–7 (1970).

Oswald, A., C. Dyer, and M. Barber, *The Creation of Monuments: Neolithic Causewayed Enclosures in the British Isles* (Swindon: English Heritage, 2001).

Parker Pearson, M., J. Pollard, J. Thomas, and K. Welham, 'Newhenge' in *British Archaeology* 110, pp. 15–2 (2010).

Parrinder, G., 'Ghosts' in *The Encyclopaedia of Religion: Volume 5*, ed. M. Eliade, pp. 547–50 (London: Collier-Macmillan, 1987).

Pearson, J. L., *Shamanism and the Ancient Mind* (Oxford: Altamira Press, 2002).

Pollard, J., and M. Gillings, 'The World of the Grey Wethers' in *Materialitas*, ed. B. O'Connor, G. Cooney, and J. Chapman, pp. 29-41 (Oxford: Oxbow, 2009).

Pollard, J., and A. Reynolds, *Avebury: The Biography of a Landscape* (Stroud: Tempus, 2002).

Quinell, H., 'The Local Character of the Devon Bronze Age and Its Interpretation in the 1980s' in *The Proceedings of the Devon Archaeological Society* 46, pp. 1-12 (1988).

Randsborg, K., 'Kivic: Archaeology and Iconography' in *Acta Archaeologica Academiae Scientarum* 64.1, pp. 1–147 (1993).

Richards, C., 'Henges and Water: Towards an Elemental Understanding of Monumentality and Landscape in Late Neolithic Britain' in *Journal of Material Culture* 1 (3), pp. 313–36 (1996).

Ripinsky-Naxon, M., *The Nature of Shamanism: Substance and Function of a Religious Metaphor* (Albany: State University of New York Press, 1993).

Rudgley, R., *The Encyclopaedia of Psychoactive Substances* (London: Little, Brown & Co., 1998).

Ruggles, C., *Astronomy in Prehistoric Britain and Ireland* (London: Yale University Press, 1999).

Smith, B. A., and A. A. Walker, *Rock Art and Ritual: Interpreting the Prehistoric Landscapes of the North York Moors* (Stroud: Tempus, 2008).

Stukeley, W., *Stonehenge: A Temple Restor'd to the British Druids* (London, 1740).

Thomas, J., *Understanding the Neolithic* (London: Routledge, 1999).

Tilley, C., *A Phenomenology of Landscape* (Oxford: Berg, 1994).

Watson, J. L., 'Of Flesh and Bones: The Management of Death Pollution in Cantonese Society' in *Death and the Regeneration of Life*, ed. M. Bloch and J. Parry, pp. 155–86 (Cambridge University Press, 1982).

Conclusion to Part Four

Much of this book has looked at rock art in the open landscape. In this section, however, we have looked at links and changes through part of our Neolithic in an attempt to determine which factors were of fundamental importance and how these may be reflected in the rock art. It is established that the shared iconography of passage grave art, Grooved Ware (Barclay 1999, 19) and other related items (see Longworth 1999, 83; Smith and Walker 2008, 50) differs significantly from the open-air art discussed elsewhere in this and other volumes (see Beckensall 1999; Bradley 2007). The construction of Newgrange and Knowth are roughly contemporary with the early phases of Stonehenge and Avebury. All these coincide with the introduction of Grooved Ware. This ceramic style, noted for its association with ritual, often as votive deposits in pits or hollows, has been found within enclosures, avenues and monuments associated with Avebury and Stonehenge, and also the Boyne Valley complex (Longworth 1999). Mike Parker Pearson considers Woodhenge and Durrington Walls to be locations where ritual feasting on pig took place relating to funerary practices acted at nearby Stonehenge. This 'complex and formal language' related to death and rebirth in the designated ancestral realm. This ancestral realm was so detached from that of the earlier Neolithic that it could only be accessed through ritual specialists who could mediate, and thus command, political power in a new social and economic order.

It is unlikely that everyone would achieve the required status for entering this realm. Quite simply, the figures do not stack up. The human remains recovered can only account for a fraction of the population, so most of the dead must have been disposed of in different ways and possibly with different customs. It seems very probable that the people who drove the cultural and ideological changes that took place in around 3000 BC also controlled who, on death, qualified for inclusion.

It is interesting that in 2009, during excavations that represent part of a seven-year programme designed to examine the association of the Stonehenge Avenue and the River Avon, a team lead by Mike Parker Pearson, Josh Pollard, Colin Richards, Julian Thomas, Chris Tilley (all cited above) and Kate Wellham discovered a site that has been termed Bluestonehenge (see also chapter five). The popular journals *Current* and *British Archaeology* both reviewed the discovery, in December 2009 and January 2010 respectively. A series of pits indicate that a stone circle about 10 m in diameter had been raised next to the river, at the avenue's terminal. Dated by artefactual evidence, the circle may date to about 300 years either side of 3000 BC. More accurately, a radiocarbon date taken from a discarded antler pick deposited on the ramp of a stone-hole after the stone's removal suggests that the monument, which the team consider related to funerary ritual, went out of use around 2400 BC (Parker Pearson et al 2010). It is interesting that Chris Catling (2009) has suggested that at least some of the cremated remains of a local population were probably disposed from the monument into the waters of the Avon. In other words, at that time and as a hierarchical social structure was developing, only the elect were chosen to be placed with the ancestors. It is quite feasible that the majority of the dead were disposed of in watery contexts on a widespread basis, as death, fertility and water are inextricably linked. This could explain the imbalance between funerary monuments and anticipated populations and why so many of the dead are invisible to contemporary archaeology (see also chapter eight).

There are two main differences between monumental art and the art in the open landscape. As discussed above, one is the iconography. The other is that rock art in the landscape is usually on earthfast outcrops. These are static, and as such were part of a landscape and had relationships with other natural features and, in some instances, celestial phenomena, even before the art was carved. The carvings created on these rocks endorsed their significance within the landscape. Selection for carving is not random (Smith and Walker 2008, 15). Their upper surfaces were exposed to the open sky. Sunlight, shadow and water animated the motifs. These stones were also rooted into the earth and could be seen to connect the earth and sky. The markings were appropriate to their context, and they most probably related to fertility and continuity at a most basic level.

Monumental art was made on stones that had been removed from the landscape. With the exception of decorated kerbstones, the carvings were inside, and therefore remote from the natural elements. The images may well have been derived from altered states of consciousness and their power was strictly controlled by ritual specialists.

It is tempting to consider that a single event may have acted as a catalyst for the monumental and ideological changes that occurred around 3000 BC. Professor Mike Baillie of Queen's University Belfast, a leading expert in dendrochronology, has shown from narrow growth rings in Irish bog oaks, and an acidity peak within ice cores from Greenland, that a major natural catastrophe took place at about 3150 BC (Baillie 1999, 51). This could have been either a volcanic eruption or the impact of a large comet. The result of either would have been an atmospheric dust veil, causing sunlight to be reflected away from the earth. The effect on light transmission and temperature would have resulted in a winter that lasted for years. To a social order that in some areas was starting to develop a dependency on food produced by agriculture, this would have been disastrous. A society lacking in modern scientific knowledge, living in a world steeped in superstition and uncertainty, would surely have believed that their 'once assured means of communication with the spirit world had failed' (Burl 2000, 30). It is perhaps possible that famine and uncertainty caused by this apparent abandonment by (or the failure of) the ancestors may have created a hiatus that allowed the opportunity for ideological change and political enterprise.

It is, however, unlikely that a single event, as in the analogy of the natural disaster that led to the mass extinction of the dinosaurs, was the only cause of change. It would seem that if an ideological change took place at that time, it took place first within societies that were already changing. These were stratified groups with developing economies and access to new ideas and material culture through long-distance contact. They were probably situated where the Neolithic agricultural package had become established.

In more marginal landscapes it is likely that there was little change at that time. This occurred when wholesale land division and ownership reached these areas, probably in the Early Bronze Age. Although the introduction of metalworking is the most obvious component of the transition that occurred around 2000 BC, it is important to note that this and other changes did not happen everywhere at once. It seems very probable that areas least suitable for habitation and food production would be the later areas to see change. Some of the changes are worth brief consideration.

Field systems and cairnfields created via land clearance associated with agriculture signify the establishment of land ownership. This was endorsed by the construction of round barrows and cairns, often in prominent positions such as watersheds. These initially contained single burials accompanied by items of material culture, possibly for use in some kind of afterlife. One of these items was a visually striking new ceramic style, the beaker. Beakers shared a similar formality to Grooved Ware but the emphasis of the often-elaborate decoration was upon a series of horizontal bands, indicating a different syntax.

It seems that at the time of these changes, the creation of open-air rock art came to an end. As noted above, the Early Bronze Age burial mounds often included pieces of broken-away stone bearing long-weathered motifs. In other cases, rough emulations were crudely made for inclusion. It was almost as if the echo of an old superstition was being carried into a new age – ensuring the fertility of the ancestors in a different sphere, now remote from the open landscape.

ADDENDUM

If, as Mike Parker Pearson has proposed, stone represents permanence and linked the ancestors with the landscape, is it not reasonable to consider rock outcrops as the 'bones' of ancestral lands? As we have suggested, the power of the ancestral dead was once believed present within the topography inhabited by the living, before ideological change driven by sociological and political change placed the ancestors beyond the reach of their unaided descendants.

Before this happened, the stone outcrops that were selected for carving were considered by the living to be points of contact with the ancestral spirits. Water and sunlight nourished fertility within the landscape via this medium. Due to their location within the immediate landscape, suitable stones were carefully selected and some were carved with symbols that emphasised their significance.

REFERENCES

Baillie, M., *Exodus to Arthur* (London: Batsford, 1999).

Barclay, A., 'Grooved Ware from the Upper Thames Region' in *Grooved Ware in Britain and Ireland*, ed. R. Cleal and A. MacSween, pp. 9–22 (Oxford: Oxbow, 1999).

Bradley, R., *The Prehistory of Britain and Ireland* (Cambridge University Press, 2007).

Burl, A., *The Stone Circles of Britain, Ireland and Brittany* (London: Yale University Press, 2000).

Catling, C., 'Bluestonehenge' in *Current Archaeology* 237, pp. 22–8 (2009).

Longworth, I., 'The Folkton Drums Unpicked' in *Grooved Ware in Britain and Ireland*, ed. R. Cleal and A. MacSween, pp. 83–8 (Oxford: Oxbow, 1999).

Parker Pearson, M., J. Pollard, J. Thomas, and K. Welham, 'Newhenge' in *British Archaeology* 110, pp. 15–21 (2010).

Smith, B. A., and A. A. Walker, *Rock Art and Ritual: Interpreting the Prehistoric Landscapes of the North York Moors* (Stroud: Tempus, 2008).

Conclusion

Prehistoric rock art in the open hill landscape was very probably created as a celebration of life and the cyclical passage of time. Throughout Northern England and beyond, the rocks are saying the same things, although there are regional and local variations in style. They may have been created as a form of religion, intimately linked with the Prehistoric Cosmos, and no doubt accompanied by ritual practices that we can only guess at. Indeed, the very act of carving into stone was very probably ritualistic in itself.

Rock art in prehistoric funerary monuments is fundamentally different, both in visual appearance and in choice of rock surface. There are examples of rock art seemingly linked with the Realm of the Dead in a few open-air contexts.

Linking birth and death, as expressed in stone, are rivers. Rivers are 'born' in hill country, the result of rainfall from the sky. Rivulets become youthful streams, and streams become rivers that eventually reach old age before 'dying' in the salt waters of the sea. Rivers were probably metaphors for the flow of life and the constant renewal of life. Perhaps rivers were seen as eternal, ever-flowing. As with the Nile in Ancient Egypt and the 'Mother' Ganges in India today, rivers may have been considered sacred.

The cycles of the sun and moon were also highly significant to both the Neolithic people and the people of the Early Bronze Age. In parallel with rivers, the sun also displays apparent birth/rebirth properties each day by rising in the east. Rivers 'die' in the salt waters of the sea, as the sun also 'dies' each day by setting in the west. The annual journey of the sun, recorded in stone, may have been seen as life-giving in spring and summer – transferring light and warmth to earth – then as weakening in strength in the autumn, before 'dying' in winter, when the sun may not have been seen for days on end. In addition, the sun, along with the moon, was used for calendrical purposes, either through precise and calculated carvings in stone or via stone arrangements. Such specialist rock art and stone alignments and orientations may also have been an attempt to ensure the perpetuation of the cyclical nature of time itself, by the act of fixing known temporal parameters in stone.

During the Neolithic, and in certain cases into the Early Bronze Age, within the British Isles, both rivers and the sun seem to have been cosmic metaphors for the renewal and continuity of life. Strongly suggested, through the structure of their funerary monuments and other stone arrangements and their orientations, coupled with certain kinds of rock art and egg-shaped 'baetyl' stones, was a belief in rebirth of the soul.

Prehistoric rock art was certainly not purely decorative, although artistic exuberance created carvings of great beauty in many locations. Definitely understood, and often manipulated for cosmological purposes, was the importance of the direction of sunlight. Rock art may well have been created as if 'painted' with shadows. This technique enabled low-relief motifs carved in stone to be best seen at designated times of day or year. Some rock art was denied direct sunlight for most of the year, particularly in funerary contexts. Indeed, there are many examples where light and the gaze of the living had been permanently denied. All were created as a form of visual language. Rock art definitely had a purpose.

These strange motifs are still discernible in stone and are still capable of communicating over the millennia right into the present, should the present-day enquiring mind commit itself to careful observation and research. If our interpretations are correct, this book (along with its predecessor) may be the closest we have come to deciphering the rock art in northern Britain and Ireland. We hope it offers insights into the prehistoric mind and how the world of the Neolithic was perceived.

FINAL THOUGHTS

It is true that we could have offered more counter-arguments, but we decided to give prominence to our interpretations, which we are convinced are part of a coherent, all-encompassing package of ideas.

In the interests of direct, uncluttered communication (as is true of prehistoric rock art itself) there can be little point in submitting readers to pages of verbal over-kill. We have clearly set out our findings and interpretations, supported by various forms of evidence, and we have referenced expert knowledge, where it is appropriate, in each field of enquiry.

Should a reader have a conflicting opinion, all we ask is that alternative interpretations be backed by some form of evidence and a reasoned argument. We would be delighted to receive such communications. At the very least, our book would have been a trigger for debate and future exploration and possible further discovery.

APPENDIX ONE

A Brief Guide to Deciphering Rock Motifs

(The following is based on our own, subjective, impressions; it is intended as a starting point for future reseach, not as the final word.)

LINKING SKY WITH EARTH

Cups alongside former courses of ancient pathways: bi-directional indicators of safe passage. Cups alongside, or within, rock-cut water channels: in recognition/veneration of water-flow. Cups surrounding, or within, basins (collecting rainfall): in recognition of water at its purest. Organised rows of cups, especially six or twelve 'dominoes': lunar month counters.

Seven or eight parallel linear grooves: lunar phase calculators; the prehistoric week.

Cup-and-ring: 'body and soul'; the purity of a raindrop in water; a birth symbol; a solar symbol in certain circumstances.

Cup-and-ring with long groove running down-slope: the birth of a stream; birth and the flow of life.

Cup-and-ring with short east- or south-aligned groove running from central cup: sunrise, birth, rebirth (east-aligned); maximum life-promoting energy from the sun (south-aligned).

Linked flow channels from cups, cup-and-ring motifs or basins: veneration of water-flow/flow of life.

Grid motifs: located at the point of entry to a 'special place' elevated above water; may have been recognised as gateways/barriers to rock art 'galleries'.

THE REALM OF THE DEAD

 Spirals: nearly always located on vertical rock surfaces, frequently associated with passage tombs or other funerary monuments; perhaps representing whirlpools, ammonites, the mind/soul turning on itself; symbolising entry into the Realm of the Dead.

 Ring(s) without a central cup: associated with funerary monuments; the body after the departure of the soul.

 Lozenges, triangles, chevrons, zigzags: associated with funerary sites. (Motifs in this category may well be the result of experiencing entopic phenomena during altered states of consciousness such as induced trance.)

APPENDIX TWO

The SIW Phenomenon

(We must stress from the outset that our interpretations of SIWs are largely subjective and relate to what currently appears to be a highly localised phenomenon.)

Until November 2010, the authors knew the locations of SIWs (marked stones in watercourses) only on the moors above Ravenscar/Robin Hood's Bay. These had been discovered following a disastrous moor fire in 2003. They appeared to mark potential crossing points where rediscovered prehistoric pathways met watercourses. We identified the network of earlier pathways by plotting the positions of cupstones and apparently associated small cairns onto a specially prepared map. The linear distribution patterns generally avoided steep climbs, boggy areas and other obstacles to travel (Walker and Smith 2006, 46–7).

Since the above discoveries, the strong probability has emerged, through our research, that the Neolithic in the British Isles saw the emergence of a form of 'water cult'. Water (and flowing water in particular) was probably seen as being sacred, possessing a kind of life of its own (see part one and chapter twelve).

Initially we considered SIWs to be route-markers, identifying the easiest and safest crossing points of watercourses. If rivulets, streams and rivers were seen as being sacred during the Neolithic, however, such stones may also have been offerings to a water deity in order to 'gain permission' to cross through watercourses. Most of the stones (there are over eight) on Brow and Howdale moors appear to be earthfast, but some may have been deliberately placed into watercourses. The shape and size of rocks and the type of markings varies enormously.

In November 2010, Neil Clark, after reading our first volume of *Rock Art and Ritual*, began actively looking for marked stones near his home in Saltburn. He soon discovered a 'portable' cupstone in the bed of Skelton Beck, grid reference NZ 65930 20120.

Unlike the SIWs mentioned above, this location is not in elevated hill country but in a low ravine approximately one mile from the sea. This stone is, however, at an obvious crossing point of the stream and therefore a probable SIW.

The rounded cobble weighs heavy, has a coarse, gritty texture and has iron particles within its structure. It measures 10 x 15 cm, and has two very smoothly rounded cups on the 'top' surface and a less well formed cup on the reverse side. The cups are all 4 cm in diameter.

With this chance discovery comes the possibility of more SIWs being found within watercourses at different locations. So far, all are at the eastern fringes of the North York Moors and approximately one mile from where the streams flow into the North Sea.

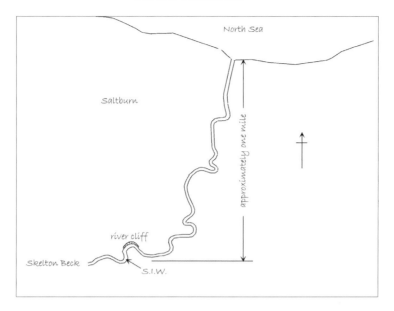

Fig. 56. The map shows the location of a 'portable' SIW in Skelton Beck.

Fig. 57. A cupstone from Skelton Beck, Saltburn.

REFERENCE

Walker, A. A., and B. A. Smith, 'By the Waters of Ravenscar' in *British Archaeology* 89 (York: CBA, 2006).

Acknowledgements

Jenny Bartlett – Ravenscar-based historian
John Brelstaff – fieldwork
Thomasin Brelstaff – hill walker
Paul and Barbara Brown – independent researchers
Simon Byers – tourist/photographer
Howard Carr – Ravenscar-based historian
Graeme Chappell – independent researcher
Neil Clark – independent researcher
Ken Grant – Himalayan adventurer/photographer
Colin Keighley – independent researcher
Graham Lee – North York Moors National Park Authority Archaeology Department
David Noble – mountaineer/photographer
Ordnance Survey mapping
Jenny Parker – editor of *Teesside Archaeological Society Bulletin*
Neil Redfern – English Heritage
Steve Sherlock – professional archaeologist
Sir Fred Strickland – landowner, Fylingdales Moors
Blaise Vyner – archaeological consultant
Lex Ward – English graduate and proofreader
Richie Wiberg – pigeon breeder

Index

Also Available from
Amberley Publishing

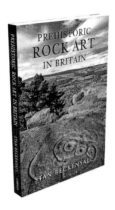

PREHISTORIC ROCK ART IN BRITAIN

Stan Beckensall

A lavishly illustrated book that suggests new ways of studying Britain's rock art.

Price: £18.99
ISBN: 978-1-84868-626-7

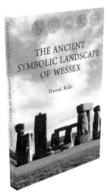

THE ANCIENT SYMBOLIC LANDSCAPE OF WESSEX

David Ride

Dr Ride explores the countryside of Wessex and investigates the many manmade structures that impose order and meaning on the landscape.

Price: £16.99
ISBN: 978-1-4456-0169-4

Coming Soon from
Amberley Publishing

Rock Art and Ritual: Interpreting the Prehistoric Landscape of the North York Moors

Brian A. Smith & Alan A. Walker

The seminal first volume of Rock Art and Ritual *will be reprinted in June.*

Price: £17.99
ISBN: 978-1-4456-0350-6

Available from all good bookshops or order direct
from our website, www.amberleybooks.com